The Complete Pakora & Samosa Cookbook:

Add Spice to Your Life with Indian Fritter Recipes!

Rekha Sharma

Ⓥ =VEGAN Ⓟ= QUICK PRESSURE COOKER RECIPE

ABOUT THE AUTHOR

Rekha Sharma was born in "Jalandhar", a small city in the Indian state of "Punjab". Her father was in the Indian army, because of which her family used to move around a lot. By a very young age, Rekha had experienced cuisines from all over India, and every time she travelled to a new area and tried new local cuisines, her passion and fascination for Indian food grew. She completed M. Phil. in English from a reputed Indian University, and then became a college professor for a few years. She got married at a young age of 23, and left her job as a college professor when she had her first child. By the age of 26, she was a mother of two- a son and a daughter, and was mostly house-bound. As she started cooking for four, her passion for cooking reignited, and she started giving cooking classes on the side. She worked as a part time cook until her kids became independent, and then she opened her own restaurant in Delhi, India. Today, she is 50+ years old, manages a restaurant, and writes Indian cookbooks on the side. She is best known for "A Taste of India", a series of Indian cookbooks.

INTRODUCTION

India is a huge landmass which contains mountains, deserts, plateaus, plains, beaches, and islands. Politically, it is divided into 28 states, and most of these states have their own languages and cultures. Even within a political state you will find multiple small villages with their own sub-languages and cultures. Needless to say, India is a land of variety, and this variety shows in its cuisine. Indian restaurants are everywhere, and if you've been through the menu of one, you know what I'm talking about.

North India is a land of flatbreads, while South India is a land of rice. India has a coastline that stretches for 7,516.6 km (4,671 miles), and you can find a wide variety of seafood here, depending on which part of the coastline you're at. Not just the ingredients, but the preparation methods also differ from region to region. If you're in the eastern state of West Bengal, you will see them prepare fish with mustard and turmeric. On the other hand, if you're in Kerala, you will watch them use coconut instead.

Majority of the people in India are Hindus, and the truly devout Hindus are usually vegetarian. Vegetarianism is especially prevalent in central India. The primary source of protein in these vegetarian dominated areas is- beans, grains, lentils, peas, etc. Indians usually refer to these as "Dal". Indian food has less meat and more vegetables, which make Indian food great for health, and also for the environment. The cooking methods used in this book make the recipes as healthy as possible without compromising the authentic Indian taste. You will find that the majority of recipes in this book are Vegan, and you can identify a vegan recipe from the "Ⓥ" symbol. Also, in India, the pressure cooker is highly popular, and hence you will find quite a few pressure cooker recipes in this book. Recipes cooked in a pressure cooker are generally very quick to make, and in this book, you can identify those recipes from the symbol "Ⓟ".

In this book, you will find delicious recipes from all over India. Most of the recipes in this book are simple, and if you're a "newbie" when it comes to cooking, this book will serve you well. You will, however, need to learn to source some of the ingredients that aren't commonly used in American cooking. If you can't find an ingredient in a local store, you can always find it on amazon.com. If there is a local Indian or ethnic market close to your home, you're in luck! Also, a pressure cooker is an indispensable tool to have in your kitchen, so invest in one if you haven't already.

INDIAN MEALS

Typically, an Indian meal contains a wet or dry dish of meat or vegetables, or both. This dish is typically eaten with an Indian flatbread, or rice. If the food is spicy, which it usually is, there is plain yogurt on the side to soothe the flavour, and also to aid with digestion. If one wishes to add a little more punch to the meal, he/she can have a pickle or chutney on the side. Salads are also quite common side dishes.

If cooking for guests, we Indians usually go for slightly "fancier" versions of the staples. Plain yogurt may be replaced by "raita" (plain yogurt with added spices and other ingredients), plain rice may be replaced by fried or seasoned rice dishes, and fried flatbreads called "paranthas" may be used. We usually offer starters and desserts to guests too.

For everyday eating, however, I will advise you to stick to the healthier low-calorie stuff. Vegetables are a staple in the Indian diet, and for good reason. A balanced meal has a good balance of carbohydrates, fiber, protein, and fat. The diet should be rich in other vitamins and minerals too, which Indian food usually is, thanks to the presence of vegetables, legumes, and grains.

Another thing you need to consider is how much spice you like. It is possible to add more later, but impossible to extract the spice once added, so it is usually a good idea to add the spice incrementally, tasting the food as you add. You will only need to do this once or twice though. Once you know what you like, and how much you can handle, go all out!

USING THIS BOOK

In this book, I will call for cooking appliances that are readily available in almost every kitchen. I understand that it is not possible to have a "tandoor" (a large cylindrical clay or metal oven used in traditional Indian cooking and baking) in your kitchen. The tandoor can be replicated by what is readily available in your kitchen, and I will clearly detail in the directions of each recipe what you need to do.

In order to prepare the recipes in this book, you will need a stove, an oven, a pressure cooker, and a microwave in a few cases. A food processor will also come in handy as it will save you a lot of hassle.

It is usually a good idea to prepare things like spice pastes, chutneys, spice powders, and other perishable basic ingredients in bulk, and in advance. These ingredients are best stored in the freezer, so if you have one, make sure you use it. Here are a few basic tips and tricks to know before you dive into the recipes:

- Read the full list of ingredients and directions before you commit to a recipe. Make sure you have all the ingredients and all the appliances used in the directions. You can make almost every spice blend used in this book easily at home, but you can also buy these at a store. I'll leave the decision to you. You can find almost anything online these days.

- A lot of the recipes in this book will call for ingredients like cilantro, dry-roasted cumin, sesame seeds, black peppercorns, ginger paste, garlic paste, ginger-garlic paste, green chutney, crispy fried ginger, crispy fried onions; fresh lemon juice; paneer (Cottage cheese), mango and lemon pickles, and some chutneys. If you want to add Indian recipes to your arsenal, and wish to prepare these regularly, you will do well to make these ingredients a staple in your pantry.
- Start the cooking process when you're good and ready, and have everything you need ready, and in front of you.
- It is always a good idea to add a little less salt and seasoning if you're not sure how much you will need. Taste your food as you go to hit that perfect spot. If, however, you do add more than you can handle by mistake, you have a few options. Throw in a peeled and chopped potato, or try eating the dish with yogurt on the side. You can also make some more of the dish, this time without the spice, and then add it to the over-spiced batch.

KNOW YOUR MEASUREMENTS

American cooks use standard containers, the 8-ounce cup and a tablespoon that takes exactly 16 level fillings to fill that cup level. Measuring by cup makes it very difficult to give weight equivalents, as the density plays an important role when it comes to weight. The easiest way therefore to deal with cup measurements in recipes is to take the amount by volume rather than by weight. Thus, the equation reads:

1 cup = 240ml = 8 fluid Ounces

½ cup = 120ml = 4 fluid ounces

It is possible to buy a set of American cup measures in major stores around the world.

In the States, butter is sometimes measured in sticks. One stick is the equivalent of 8 tablespoons. One tablespoon of butter is therefore the equivalent to ½ ounce/15 grams.

Liquid Measures

1 Teaspoon= 5 Millilitres

1 Tablespoon = 14 millilitres

2 Tablespoons= 1 Fluid Ounce

Solid Measures

1 Ounce= 28 Grams

16 Ounces= 1 Pound

INDIAN SPICES AND SEASONINGS

"Spicy" is the first thing that comes to mind when we think of Indian food, and for good reason. Historically, Indian spices have been one of India's greatest exported commodities. Indian spices go best with all kinds of food! Go out there and play around! In this section, we will look at a few of the most popular spices. If you cannot find a particular spice in a nearby store, you will surely find it online on amazon.com.

AJWAIN SEEDS

Ajwain, ajowan, or Trachyspermum ammi—also known as ajowan caraway, bishop's weed, or carom—is an annual herb in the family Apiaceae. Both the leaves and the seed-like fruit of the plant are fit for consumption. The name "bishop's weed" also is a common name for other plants. These tiny brown or green-brown, ridged, celery seed look-alikes seem fragrance-free at first, but when crushed, they emit an intense and highly aromatic, thyme-like aroma, which calms down once cooked. When eaten raw, they have an intensely fiery and pungent bite. *Ajwain* seeds are an amazing home remedy to relieve gas and stomachaches, and are frequently chewed raw by people with seasoned tastes.

ASAFOETIDA

Called *Hing* or *heeng* in Hindi, Asafoetida is a plant that has a bad pungent smell and tastes bitter. It is sometimes even referred to as "devil's dung." People use asafoetida resin, a gum-like material, as medicine. Asafoetida resin is produced by solidifying juice that comes out of cuts made in the plant's living roots. When cooked, however, it adds a pleasant onion-garlic flavour to the food. It also has numerous health benefits such as- it relieves flatulence, enhances digestion, acts as an antibiotic, etc. It is an indispensable part of Indian cuisine. Ground Asafoetida is used in recipes. It is usually a good idea to buy lumps or granules, and grind it before using in a recipe. Buy your asafoetida in lumps (or fine granules) and then grind them at home. If you wish to buy the already ground version from the market, remember that it might not be 100% pure.

BAY LEAVES

Called *Tejpatta, tejpat*, or *tej patra* in Hindi, the bay leaf is an aromatic leaf commonly used in cooking. It can be used whole, or as dried and ground. There are two varieties commonly available: the leaves of the bay laurel found typically in the Western world, and those of the Indian cassia tree. Both work fine, but if you can get your hands on the Indian version, it will make the recipes slightly more "Indian". Doesn't matter much, though.

BLACK SALT

Called *Kaala namak* in Hindi, black salt is a kiln-fired rock salt commonly used in South Asian regions. It has a sulphurous, pungent-smell. It is also known as "Himalayan black salt", Sulemani namak, bit lobon, kala noon, or pada loon and manufactured from the salts mined in the regions surrounding the Himalayas.

CARDAMOM PODS

Called *Elaichi* in Hindi, Cardamom (or cardamom) is a spice made from the seeds of several plants in the genera Elettaria and Amomum in the family Zingiberaceae. Both genera are native to the Indian subcontinent and Indonesia. Two variety of this are commonly available: small green ones (called hari or chhoti elaichi in Hindi), and large black ones (Called badi or kaali elaichi in Hindi). The green ones have a strong refreshing fragrance, while the big black ones have a milder woody-smoky aroma. Both are great home remedies to treat and manage gas, and also for nausea and vomiting. They also work as a healthy natural mouth freshener.

CHILES, FRESH GREEN AND DRIED RED

Called *Mirch* or *mirchi* in Hindi, chile peppers—fresh green (*hari mirch*) and dried red (*laal mirch*)—are members of the capsicum family. Green chiles are usually young, and they turn red as they age. The younger greener chilies have a much stronger hotter flavour compared to the red ones. The red chiles are dried and ground into a red powder, which is a staple ingredient in Indian dishes. If you're living in a different part of the world, look for "cayenne powder" in a nearby store or online if you cannot find pure red chile powder. Chiles are great for health too, and enhance digestion. They are used in powerful sinus, cough, and cold home remedies. Just ensure you don't touch any sensitive areas of your body if you've just handled it.

CINNAMON AND CASSIA

Called *Dalchini* or *darchini* in Hindi, Cinnamon is a common ingredient in kitchens all around the world, and is commonly available in ground, or stick form. Cinnamon adds a pleasant fragrance to foods, and is great for the digestive system.

CLOVES

Called *Laung* or *lavang* in Hindi, Cloves are the aromatic flower buds of a tree in the family Myrtaceae, Syzygium aromaticum. They have a strong aroma, and a strong sweet and sour taste. They are great for digestion, and relieving gas.

CORIANDER SEEDS AND GREENS

Called *Dhania, sookha*, and *patta* or *hara* in Hindi, Coriander is an annual herb in the family Apiaceae. It is also known as Chinese parsley, and in the United States the stems and leaves are commonly referred to as cilantro. The whole of the plant is fit for consumption, but fresh leaves and dried seeds are most commonly used in cooking. The fresh green leaves have a sweet citrus flavour, and smell absolutely fantastic. These are highly perishable so use them as soon as possible, and always store them in your fridge.

CUMIN AND BLACK CUMIN

Called *Jeera* or *zeera* in Hindi, Cumin is a flowering plant in the family Apiaceae, native to southwestern Asia including the Middle East. Its seeds – each one contained within a fruit, which is dried – are a staple in the Indian kitchen. They have a strong spicy aroma, and a bitter taste. It is great for the stomach.

CURRY LEAVES

Called *Meethineem* or *karipatta* in Hindi, Curry leaves from from the curry leaf tree, which is a tropical to sub-tropical tree in the family Rutaceae, and is native to India.

Curry leaves are a staple in Indian cooking, and quite a few recipes in this book will call for this ingredient. They taste slightly bitter, but taste absolutely amazing in certain recipes.

FENNEL SEEDS

Called *Saunf* in Hindi, Fennel seeds come from Fennel, which is a flowering plant species in the carrot family. They appear long, ridged, oval or curved, and green-yellow in color. They have an aromatic pleasant taste, and are great for the digestive system.

FENUGREEK SEEDS AND GREENS

Called *Daana-methi* or *metharae* and *patta* or *hari methi* in Hindi, Fenugreek seeds are the dried, angular, yellow-brown seeds of a highly aromatic annual herb of the legume family. They are widely grown in India, and taste bitter when eaten raw. Luckily, they aren't meant to be eaten raw. When stir-fried or dry-roasted, these turn into something quite delicious.

GINGER

Called *Adrak, taaza*, and *sookha* in Hindi, Ginger needs no introduction. This juicy underground stem has a strong taste and is great for health. When buying ginger, ensure you get the fresh juicy ones. If you see any signs of dryness, shriveling, or mold, you should probably not pick that particular one.

KALONJI

You might know of these as—nigella, onion seeds, black onion seeds, black caraway seeds, or black cumin seeds. In Hindi, however, it is called *kalonji*, and that is the term commonly used outside India too, so that is what I will call it in this book. These little charcoal black triangular seeds look a lot like onion seeds. They have a light flavour like oregano, and taste bitter when raw. After cooking, however, these start to emit a nutty aroma and taste.

KOKUM

Also known as *cocum, cocamful*, and fish tamarind, *Kokum* is the sun-dried rind of a ½- to 1-inch fruit of the mangosteen-oil tree. The ripe fruits are eaten too, but the majority of them is dried into rather sticky, sour, purple-black pieces of *kokum*, a delicious spice. If a recipe calls for this ingredient, and you can't find it, Tamarind can be used instead.

MANGO POWDER

Called *Amchur* in Hindi, Mango powder is a fruity spice powder made from dried unripe green mangoes and is used as a citrusy seasoning in Indian cuisine. It is mostly produced in India, and is used as a citrus seasoning, and also to Put in the nutritional benefits of mangoes when the fresh fruit is out of season.

MINT

Called *Pudina*, *taaza*, and *sookha* in Hindi, Mint needs no introduction as it is one of the most popular herbs in the entire world. These are a staple in the Indian kitchen too, and when buying mint, ensure you get fresh aromatic leaves.

MIXED MELON SEEDS

Called *Char-magaz* in Hindi, this is basically a mixture of seeds from four different summer melons—cantaloupe, watermelon, cucumber, and pumpkin. The seeds are free of fragrance, and have a very mild taste similar to pumpkin. These are loaded with zinc, iron, and potassium, and are great for the brain.

MUSTARD SEEDS AND GREENS

Called *Raayi* or *rai*, and *sarson* in Hindi, Mustard is popular all over the world. The most common use of mustard seeds we see today is to make mustard oil, which is a healthy and cheap cooking oil which is a staple in kitchens all over the world. These are loaded with Vitamins A and C, Iron, and Calcium, making them a prominent health food. They have a very strong taste by themselves, but go well in quite a few Indian dishes, as you will see soon enough.

NUTMEG AND MACE

Called *Jaiphul* and *javitri* in Hindi, Nutmeg and mace are two different varieties of spices obtained from the same apricot-like fruit of a tall evergreen tree. Nutmeg is a wrinkly, medium brown, 1-inch oval nut that resides inside the thin, brittle, shiny outer shell of a ripe nutmeg seed. To obtain nutmeg, the shell has to be broken.

Mace is the lacy, web-like coating around the outside of the nutmeg shell. This dazzling coating is cautiously removed after the fruit is broken open, and is then flattened and dried to become brittle yellow-orange mace, ready to use.

They are both great for health, and vital ingredients for the pharmaceutical industry.

PAPRIKA

Called *Kashmiri degi mirch* or *rang vaali mirch* in Hindi, Indian paprika is the vivid red powder made from mild, non-pungent red chiles. Although made from red chiles, it does not taste very hot, and is primarily used for its color. It is an indispensable part of the Indian pantry.

BLACK PEPPER

Called *Kaalimirch* in Hindi, Black pepper is often called the king of all spices. It is one of the oldest and most popular spices on this planet. Naturally, it is a staple in the Indian kitchen, and can be sprinkled over pretty much any recipe in this book.

DRIED POMEGRANATE SEEDS

Called *Anaardana* in Hindi, dried pomegranate seeds are basically sun-dried or dehydrated fruity seeds and the flesh of a wild pomegranate tree. They have a sweet and fruity fragrance, and are a common ingredient in Indian cooking.

POPPY SEEDS

Called *Khas-khas* in Hindi, poppy seeds are oilseeds obtained from opium poppy. Poppy seeds come in many colors, but the Indian versions are pale yellow. If a recipe calls for poppy seeds, feel free to use any kind of poppy seeds you wish.

ROSE WATER AND ESSENCE

Called *Gulaab jal* and *ruh gulaab* in Hindi, rose water and rose essence are made from the petals of specially cultivated highly fragrant red roses. Rose water is basically water with a strong fragrance of roses. Small bottles of rose water are easily available in stores.

SAFFRON

Called *Kaesar* or *zaffron* in Hindi, Saffron is one of the priciest spices available out there, and hence should be used sparingly if you're on a budget. Almost all of Indian saffron comes from Kashmir in North India. It has an exotic flavour and imparts a yellow color to the dishes it is used in.

SCREWPINE ESSENCE

Called *Kewda* or *ruh kewra* in Hindi, screwpine is the essence made from the flowers of a tropical tree with narrow, sword-like leaves. Think of this as rose water with a different fragrance.

SESAME SEEDS AND OIL

Called *Til* or *gingelly* in Hindi, sesame seeds are the tiny, smooth, oval, flat seeds of an annual tropical herb. When raw, these have almost no aroma, but when dry-roasted, these develop a nutty flavour.

SILVER LEAVES

Called *Chandi ka verk* or *vark* in Hindi, silver leaves are primarily used as a garnish, and don't really add anything to the flavour. This is used in Indian recipes to make them look exotic.

STAR ANISE

Called *Badian, badiyan, dodhful, dodphul*, and *anasphal* in Hindi, star anise is the dried mahogany-colored, 8-pointed, star-shaped fruit of a big evergreen tree. It has a sweet flavour, and is an ingredient in quite a few Indian recipes.

TAMARIND

Called *Imli* in Hindi, tamarind has a highly sour taste, and is a staple in the Indian kitchen. It is rich in vitamin C, and good for digestion, fighting throat infections, and fighting mild colds.

TURMERIC

Called *Haldi* in Hindi, turmeric is a common ingredient in Indian curries. It has a warm and bitter taste, and one of the healthiest spices out there. It is a natural antiseptic, an anti-inflammatory agent, and a blood purifier. Turmeric is used in quite a few home remedies such as soothing aches and pains.

INDIAN COOKING 101

If you've never cooked a single Indian recipe in your life, this section is for you. Learn your basics, follow my guidance, and practice till you make it. Do I make it sound hard? Do I make it sound like a chore? I don't know, but Indian cooking is none of those things. Indian cooking is actually quite easy, once you get the hang of it.

There are a few basic techniques used in Indian cooking that you might need to learn if you're new to cooking. Luckily, you don't really need to do these things by yourself as you can easily find dry-roasted ingredients and pre-mixed spice blends in the market. If, however, you wish to make these on your own, I will teach you to do so, just in case you wish to have a little more control over your ingredients in the future. Oh, and I personally enjoy doing these things a lot, so try it out, maybe dry roasting will become your new hobby!

Most of the basic gadgets and appliances this book will call for are quite common even in the American kitchen. I will still list these basic tools below. Feel free to improvise if you don't have one of these, and don't wish to invest in one yet.

- Concave cast-iron tava griddle to make breads
- Non-stick or cast-iron
- Round-bottomed wok (called kadhai in India)
- Pressure Cooker
- Food processor

If you can't find these in a store nearby, they are easily available on amazon.com.

In this book, you can identify a vegan and a pressure cooker recipe simply by looking for the following symbols by their names:

- Ⓥ= Vegan
- Ⓟ= Quick Pressure Cooker Recipe

BASIC TECHNIQUES

In this section we will learn a few basic techniques you will need to do the most authentic Indian cooking.

BLANCHING RAW NUTS Ⓥ

This technique is called "Bhigona aur chheelna" in Hindi

Basically this technique is all about immersing the ingredients in water until their skins become soft, and then peeling them off. You can buy pre-blanched stuff in the market, but where's the fun in that? Where's the freshness? And most importantly, where's that Indian feel?

Yield: ½ cup

ALMONDS (BADAAM)

There are two ways of blanching almonds.

Traditional Method

1. Immerse ½ cup shelled raw almonds 8 to 24 hours in sufficient water to cover by minimum two inches. (This allows the nuts to absorb the water and soften.)
2. Drain and peel the skin off each one using your fingers.

Quick Method

1. Immerse and boil ½ cup almonds in water until the skins absorb the water and become loose, approximately five minutes.
2. Allow to cool, then peel.

PISTACHIOS (PISTA)

Removing the outer skin of pistachios is much easier compared to almonds.

1. Put ½ cup shelled, raw pistachios in a small stainless steel (not nonstick) saucepan, with sufficient water to cover by minimum one inch, and bring to a boil using high heat.
2. Turn off the heat and set aside to soften, approximately one hour. Drain and put them on a sanitized kitchen towel. Cover using a different towel (or fold the first one over) and rub on the towel using your hands. As you do this, the loosened skin will get removed.

DEEP-FRYING THE INDIAN WAY

This recipe is called "Talna" in Hindi

Yield: 20 to 30 pieces

Indian deep-frying is basic as it gets. You take a Chinese wok (or a "kadhaai" as we call in Hindi) and you pour in a good amount of oil, sufficient to completely submerge the ingredients you need to fry, you then heat the oil and throw the ingredients into the heated oil.

Ingredients:

- 1½ to 2 cups oil
- 20 to 30 pieces of food

Directions:

1. Heat the oil using moderate to high heat until it achieves 325°F to 350°F on a frying thermometer. At this temperature, if you throw in a small piece of food, it will take about fifteen to twenty seconds to come to the surface of the oil. This temperature is important, as too high or too low can lead to less than ideal results.
2. Put food pieces into the wok, without overcrowding. Fry until a golden colour is achieved, approximately one minute. Using a slotted spatula, hold each piece against the edge of the wok for a few seconds, to let surplus oil to drain back into the wok. After that, move to a tray coated using paper towels.

DRY-ROASTING SPICES, NUTS, AND FLOURS Ⓥ

This technique is called "Sookha bhunna" in Hindi

Yield: Approximately ½ cup

Basically, we dry-roast dry spices, herbs, nuts, dals (legumes), and selected flours by throwing them into a skillet and browning them in absence of any cooking fat or liquid. This process filters out the unwanted raw flavour, and enhances the flavour of the essential oils, which is what we actually need. Below we will look at a few specific ingredients that we need to dry-roast in Indian cooking.

SPICES (**MASALAE**)

Pretty much every spice there is can be dry roasted, and a few of the most commonly dry-roasted spices are black peppercorns, coriander, mustard seeds, sesame, cumin, etc.

1. Put ½ cup of any one type of whole seeds in a small sized cast-iron skillet, saucepan, or "tava" and roast using moderate heat, stirring and swaying the pan, until smoke with a strong fragrance starts to rise and the seeds appear slightly darker, approximately two minutes.
2. Turn off the heat and allow to cool down. Using a rolling pin, the back of a big sized spoon, or using a mortar and pestle, squash them until crudely ground. Or, grind them thoroughly using a spice or coffee grinder.
3. Put inside an airtight vessel and place the vessel in a cool, dark place. Can be stored safely for approximately one month at room temperature, or six months in a fridge. Roasted black peppercorns can be ground fresh before every use if you have a pepper mill.

NUTS AND SEEDS (**MAEVAE**)

1. Beginning with ½ cup whole, chopped, or slivered nuts, put them in a small sized cast-iron skillet, saucepan, or "tava" and roast using moderate heat,

stirring and swaying the pan, until a golden colour is achieved (don't let it get brown), approximately two minutes.
2. Turn off the heat and allow to cool down.
3. Use instantly or put inside an airtight vessel and place the vessel in a cool, dark place, approximately seven days at room temperature or approximately thirty days in a fridge.

Tip: Different ingredients roast in different amounts of time, and hence it is a good idea to roast different ingredients individually.

CHICKPEA AND OTHER FLOURS (**BESAN AUR DOOSRAE AATAE**)

1. Sieve ½ cup flour and put it in a non-stick skillet or saucepan.
2. Roast using moderate to low heat until it starts to look golden and releases its fragrance, approximately three minutes. Stir continuously and shake the pan regularly to avoid lumping and burning.
3. Allow to cool, then put inside an airtight vessel and place the vessel in a cool, dark place, approximately seven days at room temperature or approximately thirty days in a fridge.

RECONSTITUTING DRIED WILD MUSHROOMS

This technique is called "Sookhi khumbon ko bhigona" in Hindi

Yield: 1 cup reconstituted mushrooms

Mushrooms are commonly available in dried form. So, you will need to rehydrate them before using in a recipe. Here's how.

Ingredients:

- 1 ounce dried wild mushrooms

Directions:

1. Rinse the mushrooms, then immerse in water to cover by minimum two inches until they absorb the water and bloat up, approximately one hour. Rinse them again under running water to eliminate all dirt that may still be sticking to them. Chop and use as required.
2. Strain the mushroom-soaking water through a coffee filter or paper towels until it seems thoroughly clean and dirt free. Use it in soups, rice pullaos (pilafs), and curries.

ROASTING AND GRILLING VEGETABLES

Ⓥ

This technique is called "Sabziyan bhunna" in Hindi

Roasting and grilling vegetables is the first step in preparing quite a few Indian recipes, and you will need to know how it is done before you dive into the recipes. Below, we will look at how to roast a few of the most commonly roasted ingredients.

EGGPLANTS (**BAINGAN**)

Yield: Approximately 1½ cups of pulp from each pound of eggplant

When buying eggplants, ensure you grab the young ones. You can identify these by their weight. Young eggplants usually weigh less for their size, and have a silky smooth skin with no signs of deterioration. Also, smaller eggplants are much easier to cook than the bigger ones, for obvious reasons.

The easiest and most convenient way to roast eggplants today is to just place them directly over your gas burners. If you don't want to make a mess of your stove, use a grill too. The best way, however, is to use coals and a grill, just like the Indians have done it for centuries.

Directions to Fire-Roast Eggplants:

1. Rinse, dry, and cover your hands with a thin layer of oil, and rub them over the surface of each eggplant. Next, use a sharp kitchen knife to pierce the skin in a few places. Put over scorching coals of a grill if possible, or over the direct flame of a kitchen stove burner(coat the lowermost plate using aluminium

foil), and roast, rotating using kitchen tonga as the sides turn black, until the eggplant is very soft and the skin is thoroughly charred, approximately five to seven minutes. Move to a container and allow to cool down.

2. Once cool sufficient to hold, peel off and discard the charred skin. You will have to wash your fingers multiple times as you do this. Do not rinse the eggplants. Mash the pulp using your hands or a fork until fairly smooth but still lumpy. Do not make a fully smooth purée; a little texture is required. Strain and stir in any juices that may have collected in the container. Store in the fridge for approximately five days or approximately four months in the freezer.

Directions to Oven-Roast Eggplants:

1. Slightly oil and pierce the skin in a few places using the tip of a knife and bake using an oven pre-heated to 400°F until the eggplants become soft, approximately thirty to forty minutes. You can wrap them using an aluminium foil prior to baking.

Directions to Broil Eggplants:

1. Cut into half along the length and place, skin side up, on a baking tray coated using aluminium foil.
2. Broil 8 to 10 inches from the heat source until the eggplants become soft and the skin seems charred.

BELL PEPPERS (SHIMLA MIRCH)

Yield: Approximately ⅔ cup of pulp from each pound of pepper

Bell peppers are a common ingredient in the Indian kitchen, and taste absolutely amazing when roasted.

Directions to Fire-Roast Bell Peppers:

1. Put whole bell peppers, if possible over the scorching coals of a grill or over the direct flame of the kitchen stove (coat the lowermost plate using aluminium foil) and roast, rotating using kitchen tonga as the sides turn black, until the skin is mildly charred, approximately two to three minutes. (There is no need to oil the bell peppers or poke any holes in them, or to char them completely.)

2. Move to a container, cover or seal using an air-tight bag, and allow to sit for approximately fifteen minutes. This enables the peppers to sweat and cool down, making them simple to peel. Peel the peppers, eliminating as much of the burned skin as possible. You may leave some mildly charred skin on for flavour. Do not rinse them using water. Rinse your hands as required. Eliminate the stems and seeds and chop or purée the peppers; if any juice has accumulated in the container, strain it and add it to the purée.

Directions to Oven-Roast Bell Peppers:

1. Rinse, dry, and cut each bell pepper into halves or quarters, lengthwise. Put on a baking sheet, with the cut side down. Put the sheet on the center rack of the oven, start the broiler, and roast until charred, approximately eight to ten minutes. Flip over once.
2. Put ¼ cup water on the baking sheet to dissolve most of the browned juice and use it in soups, rice, breads, or vegetables.

To Broil Bell Peppers

1. Rinse, dry, and seed the bell peppers, then cut them into 1-inch or larger pieces.
2. Put on a baking sheet coated using aluminium foil.
3. Broil 4 to 5 inches from the heat source, flipping over once or twice until the pieces are mildly charred.

SLIVERING BLANCHED NUTS Ⓥ

This technique is called "Mavae kaatna" in Hindi

Yield: ½ cup

You can buy slivered blanched nuts from the market, but these are done using machines. If you have some free time on your hands, then use your hands. This is a great exercise for improving your hand-eye coordination, and you will get much better and thinner shreds as compared to the mechanical versions.

1. Begin with 1 cup blanched almonds, pistachio, or other nuts.
2. Grab a paring knife in your dominant hand, and hold each nut, one at a time, between the thumb and forefinger of your other hand.

3. Scrape softly lengthwise using a sharp paring knife in tiny top-to-bottom movements.
4. As you do this, frail slivers or shavings will fall from the nut.

SPROUTING BEANS AND SEEDS Ⓥ

This technique is called "Sookhi dalonko phutana" in Hindi

Yield: Approximately 4 cups

Sprouted beans are one of the healthiest ingredients on the planet. Here's how to sprout beans the Indian way.

Ingredients:

- 1 cup any variety whole beans and seeds, picked over and washed
- 1 thick kitchen towel

Directions:

1. Immerse the beans overnight, in water to cover by minimum two inches.
2. Drain thoroughly, cover the container using a lid, then cover using a thick kitchen towel and put in a warm spot in the kitchen like a closet.
3. Check at least once per day and stir them a little if you wish to. Keep the beans mildly moist at all times. If the inside surface of the lid has tiny droplets of water on it, the moisture is right, and the beans should sprout in two to three days.

BASIC INGREDIENTS

Before we start with the recipes, you need to acquaint yourself with a few of the most common ingredients in Indian cooking what you might not have used before.

COCONUT MILK Ⓥ

This recipe is called "Nariyal doodh" in Hindi

Yield: 1 cup thick coconut milk

Coconut milk is different from coconut water. You can buy this in a store, or make your own. Here's how:

Ingredients:

- 1 cup hot water
- 1½ cups grated fresh coconut meat

Directions:

1. Using a food processor or a blender, combine and pulse the coconut and ½ cup of the water until thoroughly smooth. Allow the processed coconut to soak in this water for approximately half an hour. Next, pass the whole thing through the fine mesh of a food mill or a strainer.
2. Put the leftover coconut back into your food processor. Put in the rest of the ½ cup water, then process and strain once more. Combine with the first coconut milk. Add water till your desired consistency is achieved. Use instantly, or store in the fridge for approximately 4 days or freeze for no more than sixty days.

CRISPY CHICKPEA BATTER DROPS Ⓥ

This recipe is called "Boondi" in Hindi

Yield: Approximately 1½ cups

You can buy these ready-made from Indian stores, but you can also make your own. These go great with yogurt!

Ingredients:

- ¼ teaspoon salt, or to taste
- ½ cup water, or as required

- ⅔ cup chickpea flour, sifted
- 1 cup peanut oil for deep frying
- A scant pinch baking soda

Directions:

1. In a container, combine the chickpea flour, salt and baking soda. Put in the water and whisk to make a smooth and creamy batter. Let sit for about ten minutes then whisk once more.
2. Take a small wok, or saucepan, or kadhaai, pour oil into it and heat using moderate to high heat until it achieves 325°F to 350°F on a frying thermometer or until a drop of the batter surges to the surface of the oil almost instantly. Hold a round spatula with holes over the oil and progressively pour the batter through the holes, while shaking and tapping the spatula to ensure the batter falls as drops into the hot oil. Stop pouring when the wok appears to have sufficient drops.
3. Fry one batch until a golden colour is achieved, approximately forty to fifty seconds, then move the drops with another slotted spatula to a tray coated using paper towels, before you start the next batch. Keep doing it till all the batter has been used. Allow to cool, then store in an airtight vessel in the fridge for approximately three months or in the freezer about six months.

CRISPY FRIED FRESH GINGER Ⓥ

This recipe is called "Bhuna adrak" in Hindi

Yield: Approximately 1 cup

Ginger is a great garnish and a flavour booster!

Ingredients:

- ½ pound fresh ginger, peeled and cut into thin matchsticks
- ½ teaspoon salt, or to taste
- 1½ cups peanut oil or melted ghee for deep-frying

Directions:

1. Heat the oil in a big wok or saucepan using moderate to high heat until it achieves 325°F to 350°F on a frying thermometer. (Put a small piece of ginger into the hot oil. If it takes about fifteen to twenty seconds before it rises to the top, the oil is hot enough to proceed with the frying.) Put in the ginger in 1 or 2 batches and fry, stirring and reducing the heat if required, until rich gold in color, three to five minutes per batch.
2. Try to leave behind as much oil as you can in the wok as you take out the ginger using a slotted spoon to a container, toss with salt, and allow to sit until crunchy and cool. Move to an airtight vessel and place in your fridge for a maximum of sixty days.

CRISPY FRIED ONIONS Ⓥ

This recipe is called "Bhuna pyaz" in Hindi

Yield: Approximately 3 cups

These are great for garnish, and a great addition to the curries.

Ingredients:

- 1½ cups peanut oil for deep frying
- 6 to 8 small onions, cut in half along the length and thinly chopped

Directions:

1. Heat the oil in a big wok or saucepan using moderate to high heat until it achieves 325°F to 350°F on a frying thermometer. (Place a small piece of onion into the hot oil. If it takes about fifteen to twenty seconds before it rises to the top, the oil is hot enough to proceed with the frying.) Put in the onions in 1 or 2 batches and fry, stirring and reducing the heat if required, until deep brown, approximately five to seven minutes per batch.
2. Try to leave behind as much oil as you can in the wok as you take out the onions using a slotted spoon to paper towels and allow to sit until crunchy and cool. Move to an airtight vessel and place in your fridge for a maximum of sixty days.

HOMEMADE YOGURT

This recipe is called "Ghar ki dahi" in Hindi

Yield: Approximately 4 cups

If you're buying all your yogurt from a store, you don't know what you're missing out. Fresh homemade yogurt tastes absolutely amazing, is more nutritious, is free of preservatives, and the feeling you get when you make yogurt is great. You just have to do it once to know what I'm talking about.

All you need to make it is some milk and a starter. The starter can be store-bought yogurt with live cultures or yogurt from a prior homemade batch. Depending on your personal taste and diet restrictions, you can choose any kind of milk too.

Ingredients:

- 1 or 2 large, thick kitchen towels
- 1 pot holder
- 2 tablespoons plain yogurt, non-fat or any kind, with active culture
- 4 cups milk

Directions:

1. Bring the milk to a boil, stirring regularly using a metal spatula in a heavy aluminium saucepan to avoid burning the milk. You can also do this using a microwave.
2. Move to a yogurt pot (if possible ceramic, though any vessel will do), and cool until the milk registers 118°F to 120°F on a thermometer.
3. Mix in the yogurt starter and cover loosely using a loosely fitting lid.
4. Place a pot holder on a shelf in a kitchen cabinet. Put the yogurt pot on top of the pot holder, fold the towels in half and cover the yogurt pot tightly on every side. This insulates the pot and helps maintain the perfect temperature essential for the proliferation of the yogurt bacteria. You can achieve the same result by placing the yogurt pot in a deactivated gas oven using a small pilot light.
5. Let the milk rest without interruption for three to four hours.
6. Remove the lid and see if the yogurt is firm—kind of like gelatin. If you see a layer of water over the yogurt, let is be for now. You can remove it after

chilling. Once the yogurt is set, place it in your fridge instantly. If you allow yogurt to sit at room temperature for too long, it will develop a sour taste.

INDIAN CLARIFIED BUTTER

This recipe is called "Ghee" in Hindi

Ghee is a class of clarified butter that originated in ancient India. It is commonly used in cuisine of the Indian subcontinent, Middle Eastern cuisine, Southeast Asian cuisine, traditional medicine, and religious rituals. Ghee has an amazing fragrance, and red chilli powder fried in ghee has an aroma out of this world. Try it out! Although delicious, it is pure fat, so use in moderation. It is easily available online and in grocery stores, but you can also make your own. Here's how:

Yield: Approximately 2 cups

Ingredients:

- 1 pound unsalted butter
- One 1-foot-square piece of fine muslin or 4 layers of cheesecloth

Directions:

1. Put the butter in a heavy, moderate-sized saucepan and simmer, stirring intermittently, using moderate to low heat until the milk solids turn golden and settle to the bottom of the pan, 15 to 20 minutes. Initially the butter will start to froth, but as it simmers, the foaming will settle. After this, pass everything through the cheesecloth or a fine-mesh strainer into a sanitized jar.
2. Do not throw away the leftover milk solids. Store them at room temperature around two days or in the fridge for approximately six months. Or mix with whole-wheat flour to make paranthas (griddle-fried breads) or add to soups, rice, and steamed vegetables for flavour.

Feel free to add any or all of the following ingredients into the ghee to tweak its flavour.

- ¼ cup minced fresh mint leaves
- ½ cup minced fresh curry leaves plus ¼ teaspoon ground asafoetida
- 1 tablespoon crudely chopped garlic

- 1 teaspoon black peppercorns and 1 teaspoon ajwain seeds
- 1 teaspoon dried fenugreek leaves
- 2 tablespoons peeled and minced fresh ginger
- 2 teaspoons cumin seeds, 2 black cardamom pods, crushed lightly to break the skin, and 2 (1-inch) sticks cinnamon

---

PANEER CHEESE

This recipe is called "Paneer" in Hindi

Yield: 8 ounces or approximately 30 1¼-inch pieces

Basically, this is Indian cottage cheese. It is easily available in Indian markets, and is one of the most delicious ingredients vegetarians get to enjoy. You can easily make this at home. Here's how:

Ingredients:

- ½ gallon lowfat or whole milk
- 1 (2-foot-square) piece of fine muslin or 4 layers of cheesecloth
- 2 cups plain yogurt, non-fat or any kind, whisked until the desired smoothness is achieved, or ¼ cup fresh lemon juice, or a mixture of both

Directions:

1. Put the milk in a big and heavy saucepan and bring to a boil, stirring slowly, using high heat. Before the milk boils and the bubbles spill over, stir in the yogurt or the lemon juice, and carry on stirring until the milk curdles and separates into curds and whey, approximately a minute or two. Turn off the heat.
2. Cover a big pan using the muslin or cheesecloth and pour the curdled milk over it. The whey should drain through the cloth into the pan, and the curdled paneer cheese is left behind in the cloth.
3. While the paneer cheese is still inside it, pick up the cloth from the pan and fasten the ends of the cloth around the kitchen faucet to drain, ensuring that the cheese is a few inches over the bottom of the sink. let drain three to five minutes.

4. Take out of the faucet and carefully twist the cloth tightly around the cheese, then place the cheese between two salad-size plates (or any other flat surfaces), with the fastened cloth edges placed to one side, out of the way. Put a big pan of water on the top plate and allow the cheese to drain further, approximately ten to twelve minutes.

5. Take paneer cheese out, cut into shapes and sizes you want and use as required. Store in an airtight vessel in the fridge 4 to five days or freeze for no more than 4 months.

YOGURT CHEESE

This recipe is called "Dahi ka paneer" in Hindi

Yield: Approximately 2 cups

Yogurt cheese is basically highly condensed, almost cheese-like yogurt. Here's how we do it:

Ingredients:

- 1 (2-foot-square) piece of fine muslin or 4 layers of cheesecloth
- 1 (32-ounce) vessel non-fat plain yogurt

Directions:

1. Put yogurt in the muslin or cheesecloth, then twist the cloth tightly around the cheese and tie the ends of the cloth around the kitchen faucet, ensuring that the yogurt is a few inches above the bottom of the sink. let drain 4 to 6 hours. The cheese is now ready to be used.

2. Or, set a large colander or fine-mesh strainer into a large container (to catch the whey), and line it with muslin or 4 layers of cheesecloth. Put the yogurt in the strainer and let drain for four to six hours in a fridge.

BASIC SPICE BLENDS

Getting the seasoning right is a vital component of Indian cooking. You can buy readymade Indian spice blends in the market, and these are usually high in quality and taste. As a beginner, feel free to buy readymade spice blends. As you start to become more proficient in Indian cooking, however, you yourself will desire more control over how the final recipe tastes. You cannot tweak the amount of salt in a readymade curry powder, but if you make your own, the possibilities are endless.

So, in this section, we will take a look at a few of the most extensively used Indian spice blends. We will learn the basic ingredients used in them, and the directions you will need to follow to make these at your home. Once you get used to making these basic spice blends, feel free to play around and create your own spice blends, tailored exactly to your and your family's tastes!

CURRY POWDERS

Curries are the quintessence of Indian food. Curries are usually a blend of wet and dry ingredients. Wet ingredients are usually ground juicy ingredients like tomatoes, ginger, onions, etc. The dried ingredients are the spices, herbs, nuts, etc. These dry ingredients are the primary tastemakers, and we will take a look at these in this section.

BASIC CURRY POWDER Ⓥ

This recipe is called "Kari ka masala" in Hindi

Yield: Approximately 1½ cups

Buy this from a local Indian store, or online. However, it is more fun to make your own!

Ingredients:

- ⅓ cup ground cumin seeds
- 1 cup ground coriander seeds
- 1 tablespoon ground cayenne pepper (not compulsory)
- 1 tablespoon ground dried fenugreek leaves
- 1 tablespoon ground paprika
- 2 tablespoons ground turmeric

Directions:

1. Add all the spices to a container and stir using a spoon until they get blended.
2. Put inside an airtight vessel and place the vessel in a cool, dark place, approximately thirty days at room temperature or approximately one year in a fridge.

SPICED BASIC CURRY POWDER Ⓥ

This recipe is called "Kari ka masala" in Hindi

Yield: Approximately 2 cups

Basic curry powder we saw above, but with some extra flavour.

Ingredients:

- *1 recipe* Basic Curry Powder
- 1 tablespoon ground black cardamom seeds
- 1 tablespoon ground black peppercorns
- 1 tablespoon ground dried ginger
- 1 tablespoon ground fennel seeds
- 1 tablespoon ground fenugreek seeds
- 1 tablespoon ground green cardamom seeds
- 1 teaspoon ground cinnamon
- 1 teaspoon ground cloves
- 1 teaspoon ground nutmeg

Directions:

1. Add all the spices to a container and stir using a spoon until they get blended.
2. Put inside an airtight vessel and place the vessel in a cool, dark place, approximately thirty days at room temperature or approximately one year in a fridge.

GOAN CURRY POWDER Ⓥ

This recipe is called "Goa ka shakuti masala" in Hindi

Yield: Approximately 1½ cups

This Goan tastemaker goes perfectly with meat and chicken!

Ingredients:

- ¼ cup coriander seeds
- ¼ cup thinly chopped fresh garlic cloves
- ¾ cup grated fresh or frozen coconut or shredded unsweetened dried coconut
- 1 2-inch stick cinnamon, broken
- 1 tablespoon black peppercorns
- 1 tablespoon cumin seeds
- 1 teaspoon ajwain seeds
- 1 teaspoon black cumin seeds
- 1 teaspoon fennel seeds
- 1 teaspoon ground nutmeg
- 1 teaspoon ground turmeric
- 10 whole cloves
- 15 dried red chile peppers, such as chile de arbol, broken
- 2 tablespoons white poppy seeds
- 3 to 5 fresh green chile peppers, such as serrano, thinly chopped
- 8 to 10 green cardamom pods, lightly crushed to break the skin
- 8 to 10 quarter-size slices of peeled fresh ginger
- 8 to 10 star anise, broken

Directions:

1. In a moderate-sized cast-iron or non-stick wok or skillet, roast the coconut, stirring and shaking the skillet using moderate to low heat, until the coconut is crunchy and golden, approximately eight to ten minutes. If the coconut is not crunchy after ten minutes, reduce the heat further to prevent browning, and cautiously watch for the next few minutes until the coconut becomes crunchy. Move to a container.
2. In the same skillet, place the garlic, ginger, and green chile peppers and dry-roast, stirring and swaying the pan using low heat until most of the moisture evaporates and the mixture is golden, approximately eight to ten minutes. Put into the coconut.
3. Put the rest of the spices in the skillet and dry-roast using moderate to low heat, stirring and swaying the pan until a golden colour is achieved and highly

fragrant, approximately eight to ten minutes. Allow to cool, mix all ingredients together, and grind using a spice or coffee grinder till you get a fine powder. Store in an airtight vessel about three months in the fridge or approximately one year in the freezer.

GUJARATI CURRY POWDER Ⓥ

This recipe is called "Dhana-jeera masala" in Hindi

Yield: Approximately 1¼ cups

A classic curry powder from North-West India!

Ingredients:

- ¼ cup cumin seeds
- 1 cup coriander seeds
- 1 tablespoon cayenne pepper

Directions:

1. In a moderate-sized cast-iron or non-stick skillet, roast the cumin seeds, stirring and swaying the pan over moderate heat until smoke with a strong fragrance starts to rise and the seeds appear slightly darker, approximately two to three minutes. Put in the coriander seeds and roast until they are just heated through, approximately one minute.
2. Allow to cool, then grind using a spice or a coffee grinder till you get a fine powder. Move the mixture to a container and stir in the cayenne pepper. Put inside an airtight vessel and place the vessel in a cool, dark place, approximately thirty days at room temperature or approximately one year in a fridge.

KASHMIRI CURRY POWDER Ⓥ

This recipe is called "Kashmiri kari ka masala" in Hindi

Yield: Approximately 2 cups

A tastemaker from the Icy state of Kashmir in North India.

Ingredients:

- ¼ cup cumin seeds
- ¼ cup fenugreek seeds
- ½ cup fennel seeds
- 1 tablespoon ground paprika
- 1 teaspoon ground cloves
- 1 teaspoon ground mace
- 1 teaspoon ground nutmeg
- 1 teaspoon saffron threads
- 10 bay leaves, crudely broken
- 2 tablespoons black cardamom seeds
- 2 tablespoons green cardamom seeds
- 2 tablespoons mustard or vegetable oil
- 2 teaspoons ground cinnamon
- 3 tablespoons ground ginger
- 4 to 5 large cloves fresh garlic, minced
- 8 to 12 dried red chile peppers, such as chile de arbol, broken

Directions:

1. In a moderate-sized cast-iron or non-stick wok or skillet, heat the oil over moderate heat and stir the red chile peppers and garlic until a golden colour is achieved, approximately one minute. Put in the fennel, cumin, fenugreek, black and green cardamom, bay leaves, and saffron, and roast, stirring and swaying the pan, until the mixture becomes slightly darker, approximately two minutes.
2. Allow to cool, then grind using a spice or coffee grinder to make a very fine powder. Put in a container and stir in the ginger, paprika, cinnamon, cloves, mace, and nutmeg. Put inside an airtight vessel and place the vessel in a cool, dark place, approximately seven days at room temperature or approximately one year in a fridge.

MARATHI CURRY POWDER Ⓥ

This recipe is called "Goda masala" in Hindi

Yield: Approximately 2 cups

A delicious curry powder from Maharashtra and Bombay, the home to Bollywood!

Ingredients:

- ¼ cup cumin seeds
- ¼ cup shredded unsweetened dried coconut
- ¼ cup white sesame seeds
- 1 cup coriander seeds
- 1 tablespoon cayenne pepper
- 1 tablespoon salt, or to taste
- 1 teaspoon black cumin seeds
- 1 teaspoon ground asafoetida
- 1 teaspoon ground turmeric
- 2 tablespoons black mustard seeds

Directions:

1. In a moderate-sized cast-iron or non-stick skillet, roast the coconut, coriander seeds, cumin seeds, white sesame seeds, black mustard seeds, and black cumin seeds, stirring constantly, initially over high and then over moderate heat until a golden colour is achieved and fragrant, approximately two to three minutes. Allow to cool, then grind using a spice or coffee grinder till you get a fine powder.
2. Put back into the skillet, stir in the cayenne pepper, salt, turmeric, and asafoetida, and stir over moderate heat until heated through, approximately one minute. Allow to cool completely and put inside an airtight vessel and place the vessel in a cool, dark place, approximately thirty days at room temperature or approximately one year in a fridge.

SOUTH INDIAN CURRY POWDER Ⓥ

This recipe is called "Kootupodi" in Hindi

Yield: Approximately 2 cups

This curry powder has a mild aroma that enhances flavour, and is great for thickening those curries and soups.

Ingredients:

- ¼ cup dried white urad beans (dhulli urad dal), sorted
- ¼ cup fenugreek seeds
- ½ cup coriander seeds
- 1 cup parboiled (converted) rice
- 10 to 12 dried red chile peppers, such as chile de arbol, broken

Directions:

1. In a moderate-sized cast-iron or non-stick skillet, roast the rice, dal, fenugreek seeds, and red chile peppers using moderate to low heat, stirring until a golden colour is achieved, approximately ten minutes. Stir in the coriander seeds and stir until heated through.
2. Allow to cool and grind using a spice or coffee grinder till you get a powder. Put inside an airtight vessel and place the vessel in a cool, dark place, approximately thirty days at room temperature or approximately one year in a fridge.

GARAM MASALAS

BASIC GARAM MASALA Ⓥ

This recipe is called "Garam masala" in Hindi

Yield: Approximately 1½ cups

"Garam" means hot in Hindi, and "Masala" means spice. So, as the name suggests, Garam Masalas are spicy hot blends, and are easily one of the most common tastemakers in India. There are many versions of this available all through India. These are easily available in stores, or you can buy them on amazon. But if you want a version that suits your personal taste, learn to make your own!

Ingredients:

- ¼ cup ground black cardamom seeds
- ¼ cup ground cloves
- ⅓ cup ground cinnamon
- ⅓ cup ground freshly black pepper

- 3 tablespoons ground green cardamom seeds

Directions:

1. In a moderate-sized cast-iron or non-stick skillet, mix and roast all the spices, stirring and swaying the pan over moderate heat until heated through, approximately two minutes.
2. Allow to cool, then put inside an airtight vessel and place the vessel in a cool, dark place, approximately thirty days at room temperature or approximately one year in a fridge.

HYDERABADI GARAM MASALA Ⓥ

This recipe is called "Hyderabad ka garam masala" in Hindi

Yield: Approximately 1½ cups

If the basic garam masala doesn't do it for you, and you want something even stronger and spicier, try this one!

Ingredients:

- ¼ cup freshly ground black pepper
- ¼ cup ground black cumin seeds
- ¼ cup ground cinnamon
- ¼ cup ground cloves
- ¼ cup ground green cardamom seeds
- 2 teaspoons saffron threads dry-roasted and ground

Directions:

1. Dry-roast and grind the saffron before you begin. Next, in a moderate-sized cast-iron or non-stick skillet, mix and roast all the spices, stirring and swaying the pan over moderate heat until heated through, approximately two minutes.
2. Allow to cool, then put inside an airtight vessel and place the vessel in a cool, dark place, approximately thirty days at room temperature or approximately one year in a fridge.

KASHMIRI GARAM MASALA Ⓥ

This recipe is called "Kashmir ka garam masala" in Hindi

Yield: 1½ cups

A version of garam masala from the icy peaks of North India. Highly rich and fragrant, this version goes great with non-vegetarian dishes.

Ingredients:

- ¼ cup black cumin seeds
- ¼ cup black peppercorns
- ½ cup fennel seeds
- 1 tablespoon ground cinnamon
- 1 tablespoon ground cloves
- 1 tablespoon ground ginger
- 1 teaspoon ground mace
- 1 teaspoon ground nutmeg
- 1 teaspoon saffron threads
- 2 tablespoons green cardamom seeds

Directions:

1. In a moderate-sized cast-iron or non-stick skillet, mix and roast the fennel and cumin seeds, peppercorns, cardamom seeds, and saffron threads, stirring and swaying the pan over moderate heat until heated through, approximately two minutes.
2. Allow to cool, then grind using a spice or coffee grinder till you get a fine powder. Move to a container and stir in the cinnamon, ginger, cloves, mace, and nutmeg. Move the mixture back to the skillet and roast using moderate heat until heated through once more. Allow to cool, then put inside an airtight vessel and place the vessel in a cool, dark place about thirty days at room temperature or approximately one year in a fridge.

MUGHLAI GARAM MASALA Ⓥ

This recipe is called "Mughlai garam masala" in Hindi

Yield: Approximately 1½ cups

This version of the garam masala was brought to India by the Mughals, Muslim dynasts who ruled India for more than 300 years!

Ingredients:

- ¼ cup freshly ground black pepper
- ¼ cup ground cumin seeds
- 1 tablespoon ground bay leaves
- 1 tablespoon saffron threads, dry-roasted and ground
- 1 teaspoon ground mace
- 1 teaspoon ground nutmeg
- 2 tablespoons ground black cardamom seeds
- 2 tablespoons ground black cumin seeds
- 2 tablespoons ground cinnamon
- 2 tablespoons ground cloves
- 2 tablespoons ground ginger
- 2 tablespoons ground green cardamom seeds

Directions:

1. Ready the saffron. Next, in a moderate-sized cast-iron or non-stick skillet, roast all the spices together, stirring and swaying the pan over moderate heat until heated through, approximately two minutes.
2. Allow to cool, then put inside an airtight vessel and place the vessel in a cool, dark place, approximately thirty days at room temperature or approximately one year in a fridge.

PARSI GARAM MASALA Ⓥ

This recipe is called "Parsi garam masala" in Hindi

Yield: Approximately 1½ cups

Parsis migrated to India from Iran, and their version of the garam masala goes perfectly with meat dishes!

Ingredients:

- ¼ cup ground black peppercorns
- ¼ cup ground cinnamon

- ¼ cup ground cumin
- ⅓ cup ground green cardamom seeds
- 2 tablespoons ground cloves
- 3 tablespoons ground star anise

Directions:

1. In a moderate-sized cast-iron or non-stick skillet, mix and roast all the spices, stirring and swaying the pan over moderate heat until heated through, approximately two minutes.
2. Allow to cool, then put inside an airtight vessel and place the vessel in a cool, dark place, approximately thirty days at room temperature or approximately one year in a fridge.

SAVORY SPICE BLENDS

CHAAT MASALA Ⓥ

This recipe is called "Chaat masala" in Hindi

Yield: Approximately 1½ cups

Chaat or chat is a savoury and spicy snack that originated in India, typically served at roadside tracks from stalls or food carts across the Indian subcontinent in India.

Ingredients:

- ¼ cup mango powder
- ⅓ tablespoons cumin seeds, dry-roasted and ground
- 1 tablespoon citric acid
- 1 tablespoon ground black salt
- 1 teaspoon ground asafoetida
- 1 to 2 tablespoons salt, or to taste
- 1 to 3 teaspoons cayenne pepper, or to taste
- 2 tablespoons ground ajwain seeds
- 2 tablespoons ground ginger
- 2 tablespoons tamarind powder

- 3 tablespoons dried mint leaves, ground

Directions:

1. Ready the cumin seeds. Next, in a moderate-sized cast-iron or non-stick skillet, mix and roast all the spices, stirring and swaying the pan over moderate heat until heated through, approximately two minutes.
2. Allow to cool, then put inside an airtight vessel and place the vessel in a cool, dark place, approximately thirty days at room temperature or approximately one year in a fridge.

NEW DELHI STREET FOOD MASALA Ⓥ

This recipe is called "Papri chaat masala" in Hindi

Yield: 1½ cups

A taste of from streets of the capital of India.

Ingredients:

- ½ cup cumin seeds
- 1 tablespoon ajwain seeds
- 1 tablespoon cayenne pepper, or to taste
- 1 tablespoon ground black salt
- 1 tablespoon ground ginger
- 1 tablespoon salt, or to taste
- 3 tablespoons ground dried mint leaves
- 3 tablespoons mango powder
- 3 tablespoons tamarind powder

Directions:

1. In a moderate-sized cast-iron or non-stick skillet, mix and roast the cumin and ajwain seeds, stirring and swaying the pan over moderate heat until the spices are seems slightly darker, approximately two minutes. Move to a container.
2. Allow to cool, then grind using a spice or coffee grinder till you get a fine powder. Return the mixture to the skillet and Put in the mango and tamarind powder, mint leaves, ginger, black salt, salt, and cayenne pepper.

3. Roast once again over moderate heat until heated through, approximately one minute. Allow to cool, then put inside an airtight vessel and place the vessel in a cool, dark place, approximately thirty days at room temperature or approximately one year in a fridge.

BOMBAY BREAD-SNACK MASALA Ⓥ

This recipe is called "Pav-bhaji ka masala" in Hindi

Yield: Approximately 1½ cups

This one is from the streets of Mumbai.

Ingredients:

- ⅓ cup ground coriander seeds
- ⅓ cup ground cumin
- ½ cup freshly ground black pepper
- 1 to 2 tablespoons cayenne pepper, or to taste
- 1½ teaspoons ground asafoetida
- 1½ teaspoons ground black cardamom seeds
- 1½ teaspoons ground cinnamon
- 1½ teaspoons ground cloves
- 1½ teaspoons ground turmeric

Directions:

1. In a moderate-sized cast-iron or non-stick skillet, roast all the spices, stirring and shaking the skillet over moderate heat, until the mixture is fragrant and golden, approximately two minutes.
2. Allow to cool, then put inside an airtight vessel and place the vessel in a cool, dark place, approximately thirty days at room temperature or approximately one year in a fridge.

CUMIN-WATER MASALA Ⓥ

This recipe is called "Jeera paani masala" in Hindi

Yield: 1½ cups

This powder is commonly enjoyed mixed with water, but it can also be used as a tastemaker for various recipes.

Ingredients:

- ¼ cup ground dried mint leaves
- ⅓ cup cumin seeds
- ½ cup dried mango or tamarind powder, sifted
- 1 tablespoon black cumin seeds
- 1 tablespoon ground ginger
- 1 tablespoon salt, or to taste
- 1 teaspoon dried cayenne pepper, or to taste
- 1 teaspoon freshly ground black pepper, or to taste
- 1 teaspoon ground asafoetida
- 1 teaspoon vegetable oil
- 2 teaspoons ajwain seeds
- 2 teaspoons ground black salt

Directions:

1. In a moderate-sized cast-iron or non-stick wok or skillet, mix and roast the cumin seeds, black cumin seeds, and ajwain seeds, stirring and swaying the pan over moderate heat until heated through, approximately two minutes. Take the skillet off the heat. Allow to cool, then grind using a spice or coffee grinder till you get a fine powder.
2. Heat the oil in a small non-stick saucepan using moderate to high heat and Put in the asafoetida. It will sizzle upon contact with the hot oil. Swiftly put in the ground spice mixture and all the rest of the spices. Mix thoroughly and stir until heated through, approximately two minutes. Allow to cool, then put inside an airtight vessel and place the vessel in a cool, dark place, approximately thirty days at room temperature or approximately one year in a fridge.

GRIDDLE-FRIED BREAD MASALA Ⓥ

This recipe is called "Parantha masala" in Hindi

Yield: 1½ cups

Sprinkle this masala over griddle-fried breads or "paranthas".

Ingredients:

- ¼ cup ajwain seeds, crudely ground
- ⅓ cup black peppercorns, crudely ground
- ⅓ cup ground dried fenugreek leaves
- ⅓ cup ground dried mint leaves
- 1 tablespoon black salt (not compulsory)
- 1 tablespoon salt, or to taste

Directions:

1. In a small-sized container, combine all the spices using a spoon.
2. Put inside an airtight vessel and place the vessel in a cool, dry place, approximately thirty days at room temperature or approximately one year in a fridge.

STUFFED GRIDDLE-FRIED BREAD MASALA Ⓥ

This recipe is called "Bharvaan parantha ka masala" in Hindi

Yield: 1½ cups

Ingredients:

- ¼ cup ground dried pomegranate seeds
- ½ cup ground coriander seeds
- 1 tablespoon black salt
- 1 tablespoon cayenne pepper
- 1 tablespoon garam masala
- 1 tablespoon ground ginger
- 1 tablespoon salt, or to taste
- 1 teaspoon ground mace
- 1 teaspoon ground nutmeg
- 2 tablespoons ajwain seeds, crudely ground
- 2 tablespoons ground dried mint leaves
- 2 tablespoons mango powder

Directions:

1. In a small-sized container, combine all the spices using a spoon.
2. Put inside an airtight vessel and place the vessel in a cool, dry place, approximately thirty days at room temperature or approximately one year in a fridge.

ROASTED CHILE PEPPER AND RED PEPPERCORN MASALA Ⓥ

This recipe is called "Bhuna mirchi ka masala" in Hindi

Yield: Approximately ½ cup

This one is probably the hottest masala in this book. Use carefully.

Ingredients:

- 1 tablespoon vegetable oil
- 1 teaspoon salt, or to taste
- 15 to 20 dried red chile peppers, such as chile de arbol, broken
- 2 tablespoons red peppercorns
- 2 to 4 tablespoons ground paprika

Directions:

1. In a moderate-sized cast-iron or non-stick wok or skillet, heat the oil over moderate heat and roast the chile peppers, stirring and swaying the pan, until crunchy and seems slightly darker, approximately a minute or two. This will cause a lot of irritating smoke, so do this outdoors if possible, or when you you're alone in the house, and are willing to suffer a little by yourself. Move to a container.
2. Put in the red peppercorns and roast until heated through, without browning them. Put into the chile peppers. Allow to cool, then grind using a spice or coffee grinder till you get a fine powder. Stir in the paprika and salt and put inside an airtight vessel and place the vessel in a cool, dark place, approximately thirty days at room temperature or approximately one year in a fridge.

ROASTED CUMIN AND FENUGREEK MASALA Ⓥ

This recipe is called "Bhuna jeera aur methi ka masala" in Hindi

Yield: Approximately 1 cup

This one goes great in sauces!

Ingredients:

- ¼ cup cumin seeds
- 1 teaspoon ground turmeric
- 12 to 15 dried red chile peppers, such as chile de arbol, broken
- 2 tablespoons fenugreek seeds
- 2 teaspoons salt, or to taste

Directions:

1. In a moderate-sized cast-iron or non-stick skillet, mix and roast the cumin seeds, fenugreek seeds, and red chile peppers over moderate heat, stirring and swaying the pan until seems slightly darker and highly fragrant, approximately two minutes.
2. Allow to cool, then grind using a spice or coffee grinder till you get a fine powder. Stir in the salt and turmeric and put inside an airtight vessel and place the vessel in a cool, dark place, approximately thirty days at room temperature or approximately one year in a fridge.

ROASTED CUMIN-PEPPER MASALA Ⓥ

This recipe is called "Bhuna jeera aur kaali-mirch ka masala" in Hindi

Yield: ½ cup

This one goes great with yogurt and salads.

Ingredients:

- ¼ cup cumin seeds
- 1 tablespoon hot red pepper flakes, or to taste
- 3 tablespoons black peppercorns

Directions:

1. In a small-sized cast-iron or non-stick skillet, roast separately the cumin seeds, the peppercorns, and the red pepper flakes, over moderate heat, stirring and swaying the pan until fragrant and seems slightly darker, approximately two minutes each for the cumin and the peppercorns, and just a few seconds for the red chile flakes.
2. Combine the roasted cumin, peppercorns and red pepper flakes. Allow to cool, then put in your pepper mill. Grind and use as needed. Or, grind crudely using a spice of coffee grinder, put inside an airtight vessel and place the vessel in a cool, dark place, approximately thirty days at room temperature or approximately one year in a fridge.

PUNJABI RAITA AND BUTTERMILK MASALA Ⓥ

This recipe is called "Punjabi raita aur lussi ka masala" in Hindi

Yield: Approximately ⅓ cup

Ingredients:

- ¼ cup cumin seeds, dry-roasted and crudely ground
- 1 tablespoon black peppercorns, dry-roasted and crudely ground
- 1 tablespoon crudely ground dried mint leaves
- 1 teaspoon ground paprika
- 1 teaspoon salt, or to taste

Directions:

1. In a container, combine all the spices using a spoon.
2. Put inside an airtight vessel and place the vessel in a cool, dry place, approximately thirty days at room temperature or approximately one year in a fridge.

KASHMIRI RAITA MASALA Ⓥ

This recipe is called "Kashmir ka raita masala" in Hindi

Yield: Approximately ½ cup

Ingredients:

- ¼ cup coriander seeds
- ½ to 1 teaspoon cayenne pepper
- 1 tablespoon black mustard seeds
- 1 teaspoon salt, or to taste
- 2 rice-size pieces asafoetida
- 2 tablespoons cumin seeds
- 2 tablespoons fennel seeds
- 2 teaspoons ground ginger

Directions:

1. In a moderate-sized cast-iron or non-stick skillet, mix and roast the coriander seeds, and fennel seeds and cumin seeds, stirring and swaying the pan over moderate heat until heated through, approximately two minutes. Move to a container.
2. In the same skillet, dry-roast the asafoetida and the mustard seeds until they begin to pop, approximately one minute. (Cover pan momentarily to contain popping, if required.) Combine with the coriander-fennel-cumin mixture.
3. Allow to cool, then grind using a spice or coffee grinder till you get a fine powder. Stir in the ginger, cayenne pepper, and salt. Put inside an airtight vessel and place the vessel in a cool, dark place, approximately thirty days at room temperature or approximately one year in a fridge.

MASALA BLENDS FOR SPECIAL DISHES

BENGALI FIVE WHOLE SPICE BLEND Ⓥ

This recipe is called "Panch-phoran" in Hindi

Yield: Approximately 1½ cups

A delicious blend of five spices popular in east India that goes great with non-vegetarian curries and dishes.

Ingredients:

- ¼ cup black mustard seeds
- ⅓ cup fennel seeds
- ⅔ cup cumin seeds
- 2 tablespoons fenugreek seeds
- 3 tablespoons kalonji seeds

Directions:

1. In a moderate-sized cast-iron or non-stick wok or skillet, roast all the ingredients together, shaking and stirring the pan using moderate to high heat, until heated through, approximately two minutes.
2. Allow to cool, then put inside an airtight vessel and place the vessel in a cool, dark place, thirty days at room temperature or approximately one year in a fridge.

BRAISED MEAT MASALA Ⓥ

This recipe is called "Korma masala" in Hindi

Yield: Approximately 1½ cups

Typically used for cooking delicious "korma", which means meat braised with yogurt.

Ingredients:

- ¼ cup each: shelled and finely ground raw pistachios, almonds, and cashews nuts
- 1 tablespoon ground black cardamom seeds
- 1 tablespoon ground black pepper
- 1 tablespoon ground cinnamon
- 1 teaspoon ground cloves
- 2 tablespoons ground ginger
- 2 tablespoons ground green cardamom seeds
- 2 tablespoons white poppy seeds

Directions:

1. In a moderate-sized cast-iron or non-stick skillet, mix and roast all the ingredients, stirring and swaying the pan over moderate heat until heated through, approximately two minutes.
2. Allow to cool, then put inside an airtight vessel and place the vessel in a cool, dark place, approximately seven days at room temperature or approximately one year in a fridge.

CHICKPEA MASALA Ⓥ

This recipe is called "Channa masala" in Hindi

Yield: Approximately 1½ cups

Used commonly in chickpea dishes and curries, this masala also goes great with meat dishes.

Ingredients:

- ½ cup ground coriander seeds
- ½ cup ground cumin
- ½ teaspoon ground mace
- 1 tablespoon cayenne pepper, or to taste
- 1 tablespoon freshly ground black pepper, or to taste
- 1 tablespoon ground black cardamom seeds
- 1 tablespoon ground black salt
- 1 tablespoon ground dried fenugreek leaves
- 1 teaspoon ground asafoetida
- 1 teaspoon ground cinnamon
- 1 teaspoon ground cloves
- 1 teaspoon ground ginger
- 1 teaspoon ground nutmeg
- 1 teaspoon ground turmeric
- 2 tablespoons ground dried pomegranate seeds
- 2 tablespoons tamarind or mango powder
- 2 teaspoons ground ajwain seeds

Directions:

1. In a moderate-sized cast-iron or non-stick skillet, mix and roast all the ingredients except the coriander, black salt, and turmeric, stirring and swaying the pan over moderate heat until heated through, approximately two minutes. Reduce the heat to low and stir until dark brown and fragrant, approximately three minutes.
2. Turn off the heat and stir in the coriander, black salt, and turmeric. Allow to cool completely, then put inside an airtight vessel and place the vessel in a cool, dark place, approximately thirty days at room temperature or approximately one year in a fridge.

GRILLING MASALA Ⓥ

This recipe is called "Tandoori masala" in Hindi

Yield: Approximately 1½ cups

A delicious tastemaker for pretty much any recipe right off the grill, or right out or a tandoor.

Ingredients:

- ¼ cup ground dried fenugreek leaves
- *1* cup Mughlai Garam Masala
- 1 tablespoon ground paprika
- 1 teaspoon ground turmeric
- 1 to 2 tablespoons cayenne pepper, or to taste
- 2 tablespoons ground fenugreek seeds

Directions:

1. Ready the Mughlai masala. Add all the spices to a container and stir using a spoon until they get blended.
2. Put inside an airtight vessel and place the vessel in a cool and dark place, approximately thirty days at room temperature or approximately one year in a fridge.

GUJRATI MASALA Ⓥ

This recipe is called "Dhansak masala" in Hindi

Yield: Approximately 2½ cups

Typically used with "Dhansak", a cuisine from Gujrat in West India.

Ingredients:

- ¼ cup black peppercorns
- ¼ cup cumin seeds
- ¼ cup dried curry leaves
- ¼ cup dried red chile peppers, such as chile de arbol, broken
- ¼ cup fenugreek seeds
- 1 cup coriander seeds
- 1 tablespoon black cumin seeds
- 1 tablespoon ground cinnamon
- 1 tablespoon ground cloves
- 1 tablespoon mustard seeds
- 1 tablespoon white poppy seeds
- 1 teaspoon ground mace
- 10 bay leaves, crudely broken
- 2 teaspoons ground black cardamom seeds
- 2 teaspoons ground green cardamom seeds
- 2 teaspoons ground nutmeg
- 4 star anise, broken

Directions:

1. In a moderate-sized cast-iron or non-stick skillet, mix and roast the coriander, cumin, black cumin, peppercorns, fenugreek, and chile peppers, stirring and swaying the pan over moderate heat until the mixture is seems slightly darker, approximately two minutes. Stir in the curry leaves, poppy seeds, mustard seeds, anise, and bay leaves and roast another minute. Remove from heat.

2. Allow to cool, then grind using a spice or coffee grinder till you get a fine powder. Stir in the cinnamon, cloves, black and green cardamom seeds, nutmeg, and mace. Put inside an airtight vessel and place the vessel in a cool, dark place, approximately thirty days at room temperature or approximately one year in a fridge.

MEAT MASALA Ⓥ

This recipe is called "Gosht ka masala" in Hindi

Yield: Approximately 1¼ cups

Sprinkle some of this in your meat curries for great taste!

Ingredients:

- ¼ cup shelled raw peanuts, with papery red skin removed
- 1 tablespoon black mustard seeds
- 1 tablespoon coriander seeds
- 1 tablespoon fenugreek seeds
- 1 teaspoon white poppy seeds
- 10 to 15 dried red chile peppers, such as chile de arbol, broken
- 1½ tablespoons sesame seeds
- 2 tablespoons cumin seeds
- 2 tablespoons dried yellow split chickpeas (channa dal), sorted

Directions:

1. In a moderate-sized cast-iron or non-stick skillet, roast the peanuts, stirring and swaying the pan over moderate heat until the mixture is seems slightly darker, approximately one minute.
2. Put in the chile peppers, dal, cumin seeds, and fenugreek seeds and roast until a golden colour is achieved, approximately two to three minutes. Stir in the sesame, coriander, poppy, and mustard seeds and continue to roast until seems slightly darker, approximately two to three minutes. Allow to cool, then grind using a spice or coffee grinder till you get a fine powder. Put inside an airtight vessel and place the vessel in a cool, dark place, approximately seven days at room temperature or approximately one year in a fridge.

VINDALOO MASALA Ⓥ

This recipe is called "Vindaloo ka masala" in Hindi

Yield: Approximately 1½ cups

A delicious tastemaker from the coastal tourist state of Goa!

Ingredients:

- ¼ cup cumin seeds
- ¾ cup coriander seeds
- 1 tablespoon fenugreek seeds
- 1 teaspoon ground black cardamom seeds
- 1 teaspoon ground cinnamon
- 1 teaspoon ground cloves
- 1 teaspoon ground turmeric
- 2 tablespoons black cumin seeds
- 2 tablespoons black peppercorns
- 2 teaspoons mustard seeds
- 4 to 6 dried red chile peppers, such as chile de arbol, broken

Directions:

1. In a moderate-sized cast-iron or non-stick skillet, mix and roast the red chile peppers, coriander, cumin, black cumin, peppercorns, fenugreek, and mustard seeds, stirring and swaying the pan over moderate heat until seems slightly darker, approximately two minutes.
2. Allow to cool, then grind using a spice or coffee grinder till you get a fine powder. Move to a container and stir in the turmeric, cardamom, cloves, and cinnamon. Put inside an airtight vessel and place the vessel in a cool, dark place, approximately thirty days at room temperature or approximately one year in a fridge.

WOK MASALA Ⓥ

This recipe is called "Kadhai masala" in Hindi

Yield: Approximately 1¼ cups

A tastemaker for recipes typically cooked in a wok or "kadhai".

Ingredients:

- ½ cup crudely ground coriander seeds
- 1 tablespoon cayenne pepper
- 1 tablespoon ground dried pomegranate seeds
- 1 tablespoon ground fennel seeds

- 1 tablespoon ground ginger
- 1 tablespoon mango powder
- 1 teaspoon ground black cardamom seeds
- 1 teaspoon ground black salt
- 1 teaspoon ground nutmeg
- 1 teaspoon ground paprika
- 2 tablespoons ground cumin seeds
- 2 tablespoons ground dried fenugreek leaves
- 2 tablespoons ground dried mint leaves

Directions:

1. Add all the spices to a small-sized container and stir using a spoon until they get blended.
2. Put inside an airtight vessel and place the vessel in a cool, dark place, approximately thirty days at room temperature or approximately one year in a fridge.

SPECIAL SOUTH INDIAN BLENDS

SAMBAR MASALA Ⓥ

This recipe is called "Sambar podi" in Hindi

Yield: Approximately 1½ cups

In South India, you will be served "Sambar" with pretty much everything. This spice blend is the lifeblood of Sambar.

Ingredients:

- ¼ cup shredded, unsweetened, dried coconut
- ⅓ cup dried curry leaves
- ½ cup coriander seeds
- 1 tablespoon each: dried yellow split pigeon peas (toor dal), dried yellow split chickpeas (channa dal), dried white urad beans (dhulli urad dal), sorted
- 1 tablespoon sesame or peanut oil

- 1 teaspoon ground asafoetida
- 1 teaspoon ground turmeric
- 10 to 15 dried red chile peppers, such as chile de arbol, broken
- 2 tablespoons fenugreek seeds

Directions:

1. In a moderate-sized cast-iron or non-stick skillet, heat the oil over moderate heat and stir-fry the red chile peppers until seems slightly darker, approximately one minute. Put in the fenugreek seeds, all the dals, and the asafoetida and stir until a golden colour is achieved, approximately two minutes.
2. Mix in the coconut and stir until a golden colour is achieved, approximately two minutes. Then Put in the coriander seeds, curry leaves, and turmeric, and stir until heated through, approximately one minute. Allow to cool, then grind using a spice or coffee grinder till you get a fine powder. Put inside an airtight vessel and place the vessel in a cool, dark place, approximately thirty days at room temperature or about an year in a fridge.

RASAM MASALA Ⓥ

This recipe is called "Rasam podi" in Hindi

Yield: Approximately 1½ cups

Rasam is the second most popular thing in South India, followed by sambar.

Ingredients:

- ¼ cup dried curry leaves
- ½ teaspoon ground turmeric
- ⅔ cup coriander seeds
- 1 tablespoon black mustard seeds
- 1 tablespoon cumin seeds
- 1 tablespoon fenugreek seeds
- 10 to 15 dried red chile peppers, such as chile de arbol, broken
- 2 tablespoons cumin seeds
- 2 tablespoons dried yellow split chickpeas (channa dal), sorted
- 3 tablespoons black peppercorns

- 3 tablespoons dried yellow split pigeon peas (toor dal), sorted
- 4 to 6 rice-size pieces asafoetida

Directions:

1. In a moderate-sized cast-iron or non-stick wok or skillet, mix and roast all the ingredients, stirring and shaking the skillet over moderate heat until it starts to look golden and releases its fragrance, approximately three minutes.
2. Allow to cool, then grind using a spice or coffee grinder till you get a powder. Put inside an airtight vessel and place the vessel in a cool, dark place, thirty days at room temperature or approximately one year in a fridge.

Variation: Mild Rasam Powder can be made by excluding or reducing the number of red chile peppers. The black peppercorns may be reduced in quantity, but do not omit, because they are essential to this blend.

CHUTNEY COCONUT MASALA Ⓥ

This recipe is called "Chutni nariyal podi" in Hindi

Yield: Approximately 1½ cups

Coconut is a staple in the South Indian kitchen, and this recipe can be used to do a lot.

Ingredients:

- ¼ cup crudely ground dried curry leaves
- 1 cup grated fresh or frozen coconut or shredded unsweetened dried coconut
- 1 tablespoon ground jaggery (gur) or dark brown sugar
- 1 teaspoon ground asafoetida
- 1 to 2 tablespoons tamarind powder
- 2 tablespoons each: dried split pigeon peas (toor dal), dried white urad beans (dhulli urad dal), dried yellow split chickpeas (channa dal), sorted
- 6 to 10 dried red chile peppers, such as chile de arbol, broken

Directions:

1. In a moderate-sized cast-iron or non-stick wok or skillet, roast the coconut, all the dals, red chile peppers, and curry leaves over moderate heat, stirring and swaying the pan until a golden colour is achieved, approximately 4 minutes.

2. Put in the asafoetida, stir for about half a minute, and remove from the heat. Stir in the tamarind powder and jaggery. Allow to cool, then grind using a spice or coffee grinder until as fine a powder as possible. Stir in the salt and put inside an airtight vessel and place the vessel in a cool, dark place, approximately seven days at room temperature or approximately one year in a fridge.

LENTIL PASTE Ⓥ

This recipe is called "Dal podi" in Hindi

Yield: Approximately 1½ cups

A delicious spice blend that adds flavour and thickens.

Ingredients:

- ¼ cup dried split pigeon peas (toor dal), sorted
- ¼ cup dried white urad beans (dhulli urad dal), sorted
- ½ cup dried yellow split chickpeas (channa dal), sorted
- ½ teaspoon ground asafoetida
- 1 tablespoon cumin seeds
- 1 tablespoon peanut oil
- 10 to 12 dried red chile peppers, such as chile de arbol, broken
- 2 teaspoons salt, or to taste

Directions:

1. In a moderate-sized cast-iron or non-stick wok or skillet, heat the oil using moderate to high heat and stir-fry the dals, cumin seeds, and red chile peppers until seems slightly darker, approximately two minutes.
2. Put in the asafoetida and stir about 30 seconds. Allow to cool, then grind using a spice or coffee grinder until a fine paste is achieved. Stir in the salt and put inside an airtight vessel and place the vessel in a cool, dark place, thirty days at room temperature or approximately one year in a fridge.

PEANUT MASALA Ⓥ

This recipe is called "Moong-phalli or nilakkadala podi" in Hindi

Yield: Approximately 1½ cups

A great seasoning for green salads, chicken, and vegetables!

Ingredients:

- ⅓ cup white sesame seeds, dry-roasted
- 1 cup roasted peanuts, papery skin removed
- 1 teaspoon ground asafoetida
- 1 teaspoon sesame or peanut oil
- 3 to 4 tablespoons dried curry leaves
- 5 to 7 dried red chile peppers, such as chile de arbol, broken

Directions:

1. Ready the sesame seeds. Next, in a moderate-sized cast-iron or non-stick wok or skillet, heat the oil using moderate to high heat and stir-fry the chile peppers until seems slightly darker, approximately one minute. Put in the curry leaves and asafoetida, and stir for about half a minute. Allow to cool, then grind using a spice or coffee grinder till you get a fine powder. Move to a container.
2. Crudely grind the peanuts and sesame seeds using a spice of coffee grinder (you will probably need to do this in 2-3 batches). Put into the ground chile pepper mixture and mix thoroughly. Put inside an airtight vessel and place the vessel in a cool, dark place, approximately seven days at room temperature or approximately one year in a fridge.

SESAME MASALA Ⓥ

This recipe is called "Til or ellu podi" in Hindi

Yield: Approximately 1½ cups

A great garnish for meat and vegetable dishes!

Ingredients:

- 1 tablespoon hot red pepper flakes, or to taste
- 1 teaspoon Asian sesame oil

- 1 teaspoon ground asafoetida
- 1¼ cups white sesame seeds
- 2 tablespoons fenugreek seeds

Directions:

1. In a moderate-sized cast-iron or non-stick wok or skillet, heat the oil using moderate to high heat, put in the fenugreek seeds, red pepper flakes, and asafoetida and stir until a golden colour is achieved, approximately one minute.
2. Put in the sesame seeds, reduce the heat to medium, and roast, stirring and shaking the skillet, until a golden colour is achieved, approximately three minutes. Allow to cool, then grind using a spice or coffee grinder to make as fine a powder as possible. Put inside an airtight vessel and place the vessel in a cool, dark place, approximately seven days at room temperature or about an year in a fridge.

THENGA MASALA Ⓥ

This recipe is called "Thenga podi" in Hindi

Yield: Approximately 1½ cups

A hot and sour tastemaker with an intense flavour.

Ingredients:

- ¼ cup dried white urad beans (dhulli urad dal), sorted
- ¼ cup grated or shredded dried coconut (kopra)
- ¼ cup ground coriander seeds
- ¼ cup ground jaggery (gur) or dark brown sugar
- ¼ teaspoon ground asafoetida
- ½ cup dried yellow split chickpeas (channa dal), sorted
- 1 teaspoon ground turmeric
- 1-inch ball of seedless tamarind pulp, broken into small bits or 1 tablespoon tamarind powder
- 2 teaspoons peanut oil
- 2 teaspoons salt, or to taste
- 7 to 10 dried red chile peppers, such as chile de arbol, broken

1. In a moderate-sized cast-iron or non-stick wok or skillet, mix and roast the dals, stirring and shaking the skillet over moderate heat until a golden colour is achieved, approximately two to three minutes. Move to a container.
2. In the same pan, put in the oil and stir-fry the red chile peppers and tamarind until seems slightly darker, approximately two minutes. Move to the container with the roasted dal.
3. Still using the same pan, put in the coriander and coconut and roast until seems slightly darker, two to five minutes. Stir in the jaggery, salt, turmeric, and asafoetida, and roast until the jaggery melts, approximately a minute or two. Stir in the roasted dals, chile peppers and tamarind.
4. Allow to cool, then grind using a spice or coffee grinder until crudely ground. Put inside an airtight vessel and place the vessel in a cool, dark place, approximately three months in the fridge or about an year in the freezer.

DESSERT AND TEA MASALAS

DESSERT MASALA Ⓥ

This recipe is called "Mithai ka masala" in Hindi

Yield: Approximately 1½ cups

This spectacular green powder can be added to pretty much anything sweet to enhance the flavour, and is a great garnish for desserts.

Ingredients:

- ¼ cup cashews, crudely broken
- ½ cup shelled raw almonds, crudely broken
- 1 cup shelled raw pistachios
- 1 tablespoon crudely ground green cardamom seeds
- 1 teaspoon crudely ground black cardamom seeds
- 1 teaspoon saffron threads, dry-roasted and crudely crushed

Directions:

1. Ready the saffron. Next, using a spice grinder or food processor, mix together and pulse the pistachios, almonds, and cashews in one or two batches, until you get a crude powder.
2. Mix in the green and black cardamom seeds and the saffron. Put inside an airtight vessel and store, approximately three months in the fridge or about an year in the freezer.

TEA MASALA Ⓥ

This recipe is called "Chai ka masala" in Hindi

Yield: Approximately 1½ cups

An average Indian adult enjoys tea multiple times per day.

Ingredients:

- ⅓ cup green cardamom seeds
- ½ cup fennel seeds
- 1 tablespoon black peppercorns
- 1 tablespoon ground cinnamon
- 1 tablespoon ground cloves
- 1½ tablespoons ground ginger
- 2 tablespoons black cardamom seeds
- 2 tablespoons dried mint leaves

Directions:

1. Using a spice or coffee grinder, mix together and grind the fennel seeds, green and black cardamom seeds, mint, and peppercorns until a fine powder is achieved.
2. Mix in the ginger, cinnamon, and cloves, and grind one more time to combine the spices. Move to a small vessel and store in a cool, dark place, approximately thirty days at room temperature or approximately one year in a fridge.

BASIC FLAVORING PASTES

BASIC GINGER PASTE Ⓥ

This recipe is called "Pissa adrak" in Hindi

Yield: Approximately 2 cups

Ginger paste is a staple in the Indian kitchen. You can buy this store, but making your own is much more fun.

Ingredients:

- 1 pound fresh ginger, peeled and cut crosswise into thin round slices
- 1 to 3 tablespoons water, as required

Directions:

1. Add the ginger slices to a blender, as you might not get enough smoothness using a food processor. Pulse, pouring in one tablespoon of water at a time, and attain a smooth paste while adding as little water as possible.
2. Move to an airtight vessel and place in your fridge for a maximum of five days or separate into measured batches and freeze about three months. Measured batches can be used directly when you need to cook them.

BASIC GARLIC PASTE Ⓥ

This recipe is called "Pissa lussan" in Hindi

Yield: Approximately 1 cup

Garlic paste is easy to find in markets all over America, but garlic paste that has just been made from fresh garlic will always win.

Ingredients:

- 1½ cups fresh garlic cloves, peeled
- 2 to 3 tablespoons water, as required

Directions:

1. Add the garlic to a blender, as you might not get enough smoothness using a food processor. Pulse, pouring in one tablespoon of water at a time, and attain a smooth paste while adding as little water as possible.
2. Move to an airtight vessel and place in your fridge for a maximum of half a month. Since garlic paste has a strong smell, make sure you thoroughly seal it using plastic wrap below the lid. This will guarantee that the rest of your fridge doesn't smell like garlic. You can also separate into measured batches and freeze about three months. Measured batches used directly when you need to cook them.

ROASTED GARLIC PASTE Ⓥ

This recipe is called "Pissa bhuna lussan" in Hindi

Yield: Approximately 1 cup

Ingredients:

- 1½ cups fresh garlic cloves, peeled

Directions:

1. Heat your oven beforehand to 400°F. Put the garlic cloves in a small pie dish or any other baking pan and roast until a golden brown colour is achieved, approximately fifteen minutes.
2. Allow to cool, then pulse using a blender or crudely mash using a fork. Or just put the roasted cloves in an airtight vessel and place in your fridge for a maximum of thirty days or freeze for no more than six months. If you don't add any water, puréed roasted garlic can be easily separated even in its frozen form.

BASIC GINGER-GARLIC PASTE Ⓥ

This recipe is called "Pissa adrak-lussan" in Hindi

Yield: Approximately 1½ cups

Probably the most commonly used paste in India, the ginger garlic paste is widely available in stores all over the world. However, the fresh paste you make at home will contain no preservatives and will taste much better! Oil increases the shelf life of this ingredient. Feel free to omit it if you wish to use all of it immediately.

Ingredients:

- 1 cup fresh garlic cloves, peeled
- 1 cup quarter-size slices peeled fresh ginger
- 1 to 3 tablespoons water

Directions:

1. Using a food processor or a blender, combine and pulse the ginger and garlic until a smooth paste is achieved, pouring in water as required for blending.
2. Move to an airtight container, stir in some oil (vegetable, peanut, or olive) until it forms a ⅛-inch layer on top of the paste, and place in your fridge for a maximum of half a month or freeze for no more than six months.

ALMOND AND POPPY SEED PASTE Ⓥ

This recipe is called "Pissa badaam aur khas-khas ka masala" in Hindi

Yield: Approximately 1 cup

Used to make rich, creamy curries.

Ingredients:

- ½ cup shelled raw almonds, crudely chopped
- ½ cup warm water
- ½ cup white poppy seeds
- Seeds from 10 to 15 green cardamom pods

Directions:

1. Immerse the poppy seeds in the water for two hours.
2. Move to a blender, put in the almonds and cardamom seeds, and grind everything until a fine paste is achieved, pouring in additional water if required.

3. Move to an airtight vessel and store in the fridge four days to a week or four months in the freezer.

BASIC CASHEW PASTE Ⓥ

This recipe is called "Pissa kaaju ka masala" in Hindi

Yield: Approximately 1 cup

Great for making rich and thick curries.

Ingredients:

- 1 cup warm water plus more for the paste
- 1¼ cups raw cashews

Directions:

1. Immerse crudely chopped cashews in the warm water to cover, approximately forty five minutes.
2. Drain and pulse using a blender adding 2 to 3 tablespoons water, as required, until a smooth paste is achieved.
3. Move to an airtight vessel and store in the fridge four days to a week or four months in the freezer.

BASIC CURRY PASTE WITH ONION Ⓥ

This recipe is called "Pyaz vaala kari masala" in Hindi

Yield: Approximately ½ cup

A basic curry paste. Feel free to play around and add ingredients you like!

Ingredients:

- ¼ cup peanut oil
- ½ cup crudely chopped fresh cilantro, including soft stems
- 1 large onion, crudely chopped
- 1 to 3 fresh green chile peppers, such as serrano, stemmed
- 2 large tomatoes, crudely chopped

- 3 large cloves fresh garlic, peeled
- 7 to 10 quarter-size slices of peeled fresh ginger

Directions:

1. Using a food processor, process the ginger, garlic, and onion until a smooth paste is achieved. Move to a container. Next, mis together and process the tomatoes, cilantro, and green chile peppers until a smooth purée is achieved.
2. Heat the oil in a big non-stick wok or saucepan using moderate to high heat, put in the ginger-onion paste and cook, using moderate to high heat the first two to three minutes and then over moderate heat until a golden brown colour is achieved, approximately five to seven minutes.
3. Mix in the puréed tomato mixture and cook, stirring until all the liquids vaporize and the oil comes to the sides. Allow to cool and store in an airtight vessel and place in your fridge for a maximum of five days or freeze for no more than three months.

BASIC CURRY PASTE WITHOUT ONION

This recipe is called "Bina pyaz ka kari masala" in Hindi

Yield: Approximately 1 cup

Al alternative to basic curry paste with onion if you don't eat onion,

Ingredients:

- ¼ cup peanut oil
- ¼ cup plain yogurt (non-fat or any kind), whisked until the desired smoothness is achieved
- ½ pound fresh ginger, peeled and thinly chopped
- 1 cup crudely chopped fresh cilantro, including soft stems
- 1 tablespoon cumin seeds
- 2 large tomatoes, crudely chopped
- 5 to 10 fresh green chile peppers, such as serrano, crudely chopped

Directions:

1. Using a food processor, combine and pulse the ginger, chile peppers, cilantro, and tomatoes until a smooth paste is achieved.

2. Heat the oil in a big non-stick wok or saucepan using moderate to high heat and cook the cumin seeds (they should sizzle upon contact with the hot oil). Swiftly put in the paste and cook over moderate heat the first two to three minutes, then using low heat until all the fluids vaporize.
3. Put in the yogurt, slowly and gradually, stirring continuously to stop it from curdling, until all of it is completely blended with the sauce. Allow to cool and store in an airtight vessel about half a month in the fridge or up to three months in the freezer.

BASIC GINGER AND GREEN CHILE PEPPER PASTE Ⓥ

This recipe is called "Pissi hui adrak-hari mirch ka masala" in Hindi

Yield: Approximately 1 cup

This is a decent alternative to ginger-garlic paste. I still prefer ginger-garlic paste though.

Ingredients:

- 10 to 15 fresh green chile peppers, such as serranos, crudely chopped
- 6 ounces fresh ginger, peeled and cut crosswise into thin round slices

Directions:

1. Using a food processor or blender, combine and pulse the ginger and chile peppers to make them as smooth as possible.
2. Move to an airtight vessel and place in your fridge for a maximum of ten days or freeze for no more than 4 months.

BASIC ONION PASTE Ⓥ

This recipe is called "Pyaz ka masala" in Hindi

Yield: Approximately 1 cup

A very commonly used paste in Indian cooking.

Ingredients:

- 1 large onion, crudely chopped (about 8 ounces)
- 10 to 12 quarter-size slices of peeled fresh ginger
- 2 tablespoons water
- 3 to 5 fresh green chile peppers, such as serrano, crudely chopped
- 4 large cloves fresh garlic, peeled

Directions:

1. Add to your blender the water, ginger, and garlic and pulse until the desired smoothness is achieved. Then Put in the onion and process again until the desired smoothness is achieved.
2. Move to an airtight vessel and place in your fridge for a maximum of ten days or freeze for no more than three months.

BOILED ONION PASTE Ⓥ

This recipe is called "Ublae pyaz ka masala" in Hindi

Yield: Approximately 1½ cups

This paste is great for making curries with a smooth texture.

Ingredients:

- ½ cup water
- 1 (1-inch) stick cinnamon, broken along the length into 2 pieces
- 1¼ pounds onions, crudely chopped
- 2 black cardamom pods, pounded lightly to break the skin
- 3 bay leaves
- 4 whole cloves

Directions:

1. Put all the ingredients in a moderate-sized non-stick saucepan. Cover and bring to a boil using moderate to high heat. Reduce the heat to medium-low and simmer until all the water evaporates and the onions are soft, approximately fifteen minutes.
2. Throw away the whole spices, then process the onions using a blender or a food processor until high smoothness is achieved. Move to an airtight vessel

and place in your fridge for a maximum of five days or freeze for no more than three months.

CHILE PEPPER PASTE Ⓥ

This recipe is called "Pissi mirchon ka masala" in Hindi

Yield: Approximately ⅓ cup

This one is for the lovers of chile, who enjoy it when their tongue burns and eyes turn red.

Ingredients:

- ¼ cup distilled white vinegar or water
- 10 dried red chile peppers, such as chile de arbol, broken
- 2 teaspoons black peppercorns, dry-roasted and crudely ground
- 5 fresh green chile peppers, such as serrano, crudely chopped

Directions:

1. Immerse the red chile peppers in the vinegar approximately one hour to soften. Move to a blender.
2. Add the green chile peppers and the peppercorns and pulse until the desired smoothness is achieved. Move to an airtight jar and place in your fridge for a maximum of six months.

FRIED ONION PASTE

This recipe is called "Talae pyaz ka masala" in Hindi

Yield: Approximately 1 cup

This paste is used to make delicious rich-tasting curries.

Ingredients:

- ½ cup non-fat plain yogurt
- 1 cup melted ghee or vegetable oil for deep-frying
- 1 large onion, cut in half along the length and thinly chopped

- 4 large cloves fresh garlic, peeled
- 6 to 8 quarter-size slices of peeled fresh ginger

Directions:

1. Heat the oil in a big non-stick saucepan using moderate to high heat and fry the ginger and garlic until a golden colour is achieved, approximately two minutes. Put in the onion and fry until everything is thoroughly browned, approximately five minutes. Place on top of paper towels to drain and save the ghee/oil for future use.
2. Move to a blender or a food processor, put in the yogurt and pulse until a smooth and thick paste is achieved. Move to an airtight vessel and place in your fridge for a maximum of five days or freeze for no more than three months.

GOAN VINDALOO PASTE Ⓥ

This recipe is called "Goa ka vindaloo masala" in Hindi

Yield: Approximately 1 cup

Useful In making hot and tangy spicy dishes.

Ingredients:

- ¼ cup distilled white vinegar
- ½ cup Goan Vindaloo Powder (store-bought)
- 1 large onion, crudely chopped
- 2 teaspoons salt, or to taste
- 3 tablespoons peanut oil
- 3 to 4 dried red chile peppers, such chile de arbol, broken
- 30 to 40 fresh curry leaves
- 5 to 7 large cloves fresh garlic, peeled
- 8 to 10 quarter-size slices of peeled fresh ginger

Directions:

1. Immerse the red chile peppers in the vinegar, one to two hours. In the meantime, ready the vindaloo powder. Using a food processor, combine and pulse the red chile peppers, plus the vinegar, ginger, garlic, onion, curry leaves,

and salt until a smooth paste is achieved. Stir in the vindaloo masala and process once more.

2. Heat the oil in a big non-stick wok or saucepan using moderate to high heat and stir-fry the paste, using moderate to high heat the first two to three minutes, and then over moderate heat until rich brown, approximately eight to ten minutes. Allow to cool, then store in an airtight vessel about thirty days in the fridge or six months in the freezer.

GUJARATI GREEN PASTE Ⓥ

This recipe is called "Gujerati hara masala" in Hindi

Yield: Approximately 1½ cups

A very hot and spicy paste from west India.

Ingredients:

- ¼ cup vegetable oil
- 4 to 6 ounces fresh green chile peppers, such as serrano, crudely chopped
- 6 ounces fresh garlic cloves, peeled
- 8 ounces fresh ginger, peeled and cut crosswise into thin round slices

Directions:

1. Using a food processor or a blender, combine and pulse all of the ingredients until high smoothness is achieved.
2. Move to an airtight vessel and place in your fridge for a maximum of 1 month, or freeze for no more than six months.

HYDERABADI GINGER-GARLIC PASTE Ⓥ

This recipe is called "Hyderabadi pissa adrak-lussan" in Hindi

Yield: Approximately 1½ cups

A Hyderabadi twist on a classic.

Ingredients:

- ¼ pound fresh garlic cloves, peeled
- ¾ pound fresh ginger, peeled and cut crosswise into thin round slices
- 1 to 3 tablespoons water

Directions:

1. You will a blander for this as a food processor just won't cut it. Mix together and pulse the ginger and garlic until the desired smoothness is achieved, pouring in water as required for blending.
2. Move to an airtight vessel and place in your fridge for a maximum of ten days or freeze for no more than six months.

KERALA FRIED ONION PASTE Ⓥ

This recipe is called "Kerala ka talae pyaz ka masala" in Hindi

Yield: Approximately 2 cups

A delicious paste with a hint of coconut.

Ingredients:

- ½ cup peanut oil
- 1 cup Coconut Milk (Homemade or store-bought)
- 15 to 20 fresh curry leaves
- 2 large onions, crudely chopped
- 5 large cloves fresh garlic, peeled
- 5 to 8 dried red chile peppers, such as chile de arbol, broken
- 6 to 8 quarter-size slices of peeled fresh ginger

Directions:

1. Heat the oil in a big non-stick saucepan using moderate to high heat and fry the red chile peppers and the onion until a golden colour is achieved, about three to four minutes. Put in the garlic, ginger, and curry leaves and fry until everything is well-browned, three to five minutes.
2. Cool, drain, and save the oil for future use. Then move to a blender or a food processor, put in the coconut milk and pulse until a smooth and thick paste is achieved. Move to an airtight vessel and place in your fridge for a maximum of five days or freeze for no more than three months.

MINTY GREEN CURRY PASTE Ⓥ

This recipe is called "Pudinae vaala hara kari masala" in Hindi

Yield: Approximately 1 cup

Great for making minty curries.

Ingredients:

- ¼ cup peanut oil
- ½ cup crudely chopped fresh mint leaves
- 1 cup crudely chopped fresh cilantro, including soft stems
- 1 tablespoon fresh lime juice
- 1 teaspoon salt, or to taste
- 1 to 3 fresh green chile peppers, such as serrano, stemmed
- 1½ teaspoons garam masala
- 4 to 5 large cloves fresh garlic, peeled
- 5 to 6 scallions, crudely chopped with greens
- 6 quarter-size slices of peeled fresh ginger

Directions:

1. Using a food processor, combine and pulse the garlic, ginger, chile peppers, and scallions until minced. Put in the cilantro, mint, and lime juice and process until a smooth paste is achieved. Move to a container and stir in the garam masala and salt.
2. Heat the oil in a big non-stick wok or saucepan using moderate to high heat, put in the green paste and cook, stirring over moderate heat for the first two to three minutes and then using moderate to low heat until thoroughly browned, approximately ten to twelve minutes. Allow to cool, then store in an airtight vessel for approximately thirty days in the fridge or six months in the freezer.

MUGHLAI CURRY PASTE WITH NUTS

This recipe is called "Korma ka geela masala" in Hindi

Yield: Approximately 1 cup

Who doesn't live cream and nuts?

Ingredients:

- *2 tablespoons* Basic Ginger-Garlic Paste
- *½ cup* Fragrant Masala with Nuts
- ¼ cup heavy cream
- ½ cup non-fat plain yogurt
- 2 tablespoons melted ghee or vegetable oil

Directions:

1. Ready the paste and then the masala. Heat the ghee in a big non-stick saucepan using moderate to high heat, put in the ginger-garlic paste and korma masala and cook, stirring, until a mild brown colour is achieved.
2. In a container, whip together the cream and yogurt using a whisk or an electric beater, then add it to the saucepan in a thin stream, stirring continuously to stop curdling, until it is thoroughly blended with the paste. Allow to cool, then store in an airtight vessel in the fridge seven to ten days or three months in the freezer.

SPICY YELLOW CURRY PASTE Ⓥ

This recipe is called "Masaladar peela kari masala" in Hindi

Yield: Approximately 1 cup

A delicious combination of turmeric and red chile.

Ingredients:

- ¼ cup peanut oil
- 1 large onion, crudely chopped
- 1 tablespoon fresh lime juice
- 1 teaspoon cayenne pepper
- 1 teaspoon garam masala
- 1 teaspoon ground turmeric
- 1 teaspoon salt, or to taste
- 1 to 3 fresh green chile peppers, such as serrano, crudely chopped
- 10 quarter-size slices of peeled fresh ginger

- 4 to 5 large cloves fresh garlic, peeled

Directions:

1. Using a food processor, combine and pulse the ginger, garlic, chile peppers, onion, lime juice, turmeric, cayenne pepper, garam masala, and salt until a smooth paste is achieved.
2. Heat the oil in a big non-stick wok or sauce-pan, put in the paste, and cook, stirring using moderate to high heat the first two to three minutes and then using moderate to low heat until thoroughly browned, approximately ten to twelve minutes. Allow to cool, then store in an airtight vessel about thirty days in the fridge or six months in the freezer.

TAMARIND PASTE Ⓥ

This recipe is called "Imli ras" in Hindi

Yield: Approximately 1½ cups

You can easily buy this from a store, but make your own for better flavour.

Ingredients:

- 1½ cups warm water
- 6 ounces shelled fresh tamarind pods with seeds or 5 ounces tamarind pulp without seeds

Directions:

1. Immerse the shelled tamarind pods or pulp in 1 cup of the water, one to two hours to soften. Using your fingers, softly rub and mash the tamarind to loosen the pulp from the fibrous parts and to isolate the seeds.
2. Throw away the seeds and pass the softened pulp through a fine-mesh strainer or a food mill until a smooth paste is achieved. Move the fibrous remains to a container, mix the rest of the ½ cup water into the pulp and mash once more. Then pass through the sieve or food mill to extract more paste. Combine with the already extracted paste. Store in an airtight vessel about 1 week in the fridge or freeze measured amounts into ice cube trays and store the cubes in zip closure bags up to six months in the freezer.

CHUTNEY

Chutneys are basically spicy Indian sauces. They go great with not only Indian food, but also western food! Next time you're enjoying a steak, try it with some chutney on the side!

Indian chutneys can be broadly classified into two categories: fresh and preserved. In the fresh, perishable category we find the tangy purées of fresh herbs, spices, fruits, and yogurt. These chutneys stay fresh for about ten days in a fridge. If the chutney doesn't contain yogurt, if is safe to freeze. The fresh purées keep well in a freezer too. To freeze, pour the chutneys in serving-size containers or in ice-cube trays. Once they freeze, move to plastic zip-closure bags and freeze for no more than six months. Thaw at room temperature, or if you are in a rush, using a microwave.

The story with the non-perishable chutneys is a little different. These can be stores safely even at room temperature for long periods of time.

Ⓥ= Vegan Ⓟ= Quick Pressure Cooker Recipe

GREEN CHUTNEYS

BASIC GREEN CHUTNEY Ⓥ

This recipe is called "Hari chutni" in Hindi

Yield: Approximately 1½ cups

One of the most common chutneys you will see in India. Can be enjoyed with pretty much everything, and tastes absolutely amazing!

Ingredients:

* ½ teaspoon freshly ground black pepper, or to taste

- 1 cup fresh mint leaves, trimmed
- 1 teaspoon salt, or to taste
- 1 teaspoon sugar
- 2 to 3 cups crudely chopped fresh cilantro, including soft stems
- 2 to 5 fresh green chile peppers, such as serrano, stemmed
- 3 to 4 tablespoons fresh lime or lemon juice
- 6 to 8 scallions, just the green parts, crudely chopped

Directions:

1. Using a food processor or blender, combine and pulse the green chile peppers and scallion greens until minced. Put in the mint and cilantro to the work container and process, stopping intermittently to scrub the inner walls using a spatula, until puréed. While processing, trickle the lime juice through the feeder tube into the work container and pulse the chutney until the desired smoothness is achieved.
2. Put in the sugar, salt, and pepper and process once more. Tweak the seasonings to your taste. Move to a container and serve instantly, place in your fridge for approximately ten days, or freeze for no more than six months.

CILANTRO-LIME CHUTNEY Ⓥ

This recipe is called "Dhania chutni" in Hindi

Yield: Approximately 2 cups

A delicious chutney popular in all of India!

Ingredients:

- ½ cup fresh mint leaves
- ½ teaspoon cumin seeds, dry-roasted and crudely ground (See the Dry Roasting section in Introduction)
- 1 small green bell pepper, crudely chopped
- 1 teaspoon Chaat Masala (Homemade or store-bought)
- 1 teaspoon salt, or to taste
- 1 teaspoon sugar
- 2 to 3 tablespoons fresh lime or lemon juice

- 3 cups firmly packed, crudely chopped fresh cilantro, including soft stems
- 3 to 5 fresh green chile peppers, such as serrano, stemmed
- 4 quarter-size slices peeled fresh ginger
- 5 to 6 scallions, green parts only, crudely chopped

Directions:

1. Ready the cumin seeds and the chaat masala. Next, Using a food processor or a blender, blend together the green chile peppers, ginger, bell pepper, and scallion greens until minced. Put in the cilantro and mint to the work container and process, scraping the sides using a spatula a few times, until puréed. While processing, trickle the lime juice through the feeder tube into the work container and process to make a smooth chutney.
2. Put in the chaat masala, sugar, and salt and process once more. Tweak the seasonings to your taste. Move to a container and lightly stir in the cumin with some of it visible as a decoration. Serve instantly, place in your fridge for approximately ten days, or freeze for no more than six months.

MINT CHUTNEY Ⓥ

This recipe is called "Pudina-anardana chutni" in Hindi

Yield: Approximately 1½ cups

This chutney is a breath of freshness. Easily one of the favourite chutneys in India.

Ingredients:

- ½ teaspoon freshly ground black pepper
- 1 cup crudely chopped fresh cilantro, including soft stems
- 1 small red onion, crudely chopped
- 1 tablespoon fresh lemon juice
- 1 teaspoon salt, or to taste
- 1 teaspoon sugar
- 2 cups fresh mint leaves
- 2 teaspoons ground dried pomegranate seeds
- 2 to 4 tablespoons water
- 3 to 5 crudely chopped fresh green chile peppers, such as serrano, stemmed

Directions:

1. Add the onion, chile peppers, lemon juice, and 2 tablespoons of water to a blender and pulse until the desired smoothness is achieved. Put in the mint and cilantro in 2 batches, putting in more once the first batch becomes smooth, and pulse until thoroughly smooth. Put in the rest of the 2 tablespoons of the water, if required.
2. Put in the pomegranate seeds, pepper, sugar, and salt and blend once more. Tweak the seasonings to your taste. Move to a container and serve instantly, place in your fridge for approximately ten days, or freeze for no more than six months.

MINT-GARLIC CHUTNEY Ⓥ

This recipe is called "Pudina, lussan, moong-phalli aur imli ki chutni" in Hindi

Yield: Approximately 1½ cups

This chutney has a strong flavour, and goes great with fried snacks!

Ingredients:

- ⅛ teaspoon ground asafoetida
- ½ cup roasted peanuts, red skins removed
- 1 tablespoon peanut oil
- 1 teaspoon black mustard seeds
- 1 teaspoon salt, or to taste
- 1 teaspoon sugar
- 10 large cloves fresh garlic, peeled
- 2 cups packed fresh mint leaves
- 2 to 3 tablespoons Tamarind Paste
- 4 to 6 fresh green chile peppers, such as serrano, stemmed
- 5 to 6 fresh curry leaves

Directions:

1. Ready the tamarind paste. Next, Using a food processor or a blender, combine and pulse the peanuts, garlic, chile peppers, and mint until minced. Put in the

tamarind paste, sugar, and salt and process once more until a smooth purée is achieved. Put in a spoonful or 2 of water if required for blending. Tweak the seasonings to your taste. Move to a serving container.

2. Heat the oil in a big non-stick wok or saucepan using moderate to high heat and Put in the mustard seeds; they should splutter upon contact with the hot oil, so reduce the heat and cover the pan until the spluttering diminishes. Put in the curry leaves and asafoetida, stir for approximately half a minute, move to the chutney and stir mildly to combine, with parts of it visible as a decoration. Move to a container and serve instantly, place in your fridge for approximately ten days, or freeze for no more than six months.

SCALLION-GINGER CHUTNEY

This recipe is called "Harae pyaz aur adrak ki chutni" in Hindi

Yield: Approximately 1½ cups

This chutney has an intense hot flavour.

Ingredients:

- 1 (2½-inch) piece fresh ginger, peeled and cut into thin quarter-size rounds
- 1 cup fresh mint or cilantro leaves
- 1 teaspoon salt, or to taste
- 1 teaspoon sugar
- 12 to 15 young scallions, with green parts included, crudely chopped
- 2 to 3 tablespoons fresh lime or lemon juice
- 2 to 3 tablespoons non-fat plain yogurt
- 2 to 4 fresh green chile peppers, such as serrano, stemmed

Directions:

1. Put the chile peppers, ginger, scallion greens, lemon juice, and yogurt into a food processor or a blender and process until minced.
2. Put in the sugar, salt, and mint or cilantro leaves, and process to a smooth purée. Tweak the seasonings to your taste. Move to a container and serve instantly, place in your fridge for approximately ten days, or freeze for no more than six months.

SOUTH INDIAN CILANTRO CHUTNEY Ⓥ

This recipe is called "Kothmir ki chutni" in Hindi

Yield: Approximately 1½ cups

A smooth South Indian chutney with an intense flavor.

Ingredients:

- ⅛ teaspoon ground asafoetida
- ¼ cup <u>Tamarind Paste</u>, or to taste
- 1 tablespoon dried white urad beans (dhulli urad dal), sorted
- 1 tablespoon peanut oil
- 1 teaspoon salt, or to taste
- 2 teaspoons black mustard seeds
- 3 cups firmly packed, crudely chopped fresh cilantro, including soft stems
- 4 to 6 dried red chile peppers, such as chile de arbol, crudely broken

Directions:

1. Ready the tamarind paste. Next, heat the oil in a small-sized non-stick saucepan over moderate heat and Put in the mustard seeds, red chile peppers, dal, and asafoetida. Cook, swaying the pan until the dal is golden, approximately one minute. Allow to cool and move to a blender and blend until as fine as possible.
2. Put in the tamarind paste and then Put in the cilantro in 2 or 3 batches, putting in more once the first batch becomes smooth. Add 2 to 3 tablespoons water, if required. Stir in the salt. Tweak the seasonings to your taste. Move to a container and serve instantly, place in your fridge for approximately ten days, or freeze for no more than six months.

COCONUT CHUTNEYS

FRESH COCONUT CHUTNEY WITH CILANTRO

This recipe is called "Nariyal aur dhania chutni" in Hindi

Yield: Approximately 2½ cups

Ingredients:

- ⅛ teaspoon ground asafoetida
- 1 cup crudely chopped fresh cilantro, including soft stems
- 1 cup plain yogurt, non-fat or any kind, whisked until the desired smoothness is achieved
- 1 fresh coconut
- 1 tablespoon coconut or peanut oil
- 1 teaspoon black mustard seeds
- 1 teaspoon salt, or to taste
- 2 tablespoons minced fresh curry leaves
- 2 to 3 tablespoons South Indian Sambar Powder (Homemade or store-bought)
- 3 quarter-size slices of peeled fresh ginger
- 3 tablespoons fresh lemon juice
- 3 to 5 fresh green chile peppers, such as serrano, stemmed

Directions:

1. Ready the sambar powder. Next, shell the coconut. Next, using a vegetable peeler, peel the brown skin off the flesh and discard. Crudely cut the coconut meat into ½- to 1-inch pieces. Using a food processor or a blender, combine and pulse the coconut, green chile peppers, and ginger until minced.
2. Put in the lemon juice, yogurt, and cilantro and process, scraping the sides of the work container a few times using a spatula until thoroughly smooth. Put in the salt and sambar powder and process once more. Tweak the seasonings to your taste, then move to a serving container.
3. Heat the oil in a small-sized non-stick saucepan using moderate to high heat and Put in the mustard seeds, curry leaves, and asafoetida; they should splutter upon contact with the hot oil, so reduce the heat and cover the pan until the spluttering diminishes. Swiftly add to the chutney and stir mildly with parts of it visible as a decoration. Move to a container and serve instantly,

place in your fridge for approximately ten days, or freeze for no more than six months.

MINTY COCONUT-TAMARIND CHUTNEY

Ⓥ

This recipe is called "Nariyal aur Imli ki chutni" in Hindi

Yield: Approximately 1½ cups

Ingredients:

- ¼ cup fresh mint leaves
- ¼ cup Tamarind Paste
- ½ cup crudely chopped fresh cilantro, including soft stems
- 1 fresh coconut
- 1 teaspoon crudely ground dry-roasted cumin seeds (See the dry-roasting section in Introduction)
- 1 teaspoon salt, or to taste
- 2 large cloves fresh garlic, peeled
- 3 to 5 fresh green chile peppers, such as serrano, stemmed
- 6 to 8 quarter-size slices peeled fresh ginger

Directions:

1. Prepare cumin and tamarind paste. Next, shell the <u>coconut</u>. Using a vegetable peeler, peel the brown skin off the meat and discard. Crudely cut the coconut meat into ½- to 1-inch pieces. Using a food processor a blender, combine and pulse the coconut, ginger, green chile peppers, and garlic until minced.
2. Put in the cilantro, mint, tamarind, and salt and process, scraping the sides of the work container a few times using a spatula, until the desired smoothness is achieved. Tweak the seasonings to your taste, then move to a serving container. Garnish with the cumin and serve instantly, place in your fridge for approximately ten days, or freeze for no more than six months.

ROASTED COCONUT CHUTNEY Ⓥ

This recipe is called "Bhunae nariyal ki chutni" in Hindi

Yield: Approximately 1½ cups

Ingredients:

- ½ teaspoon fenugreek seeds
- 1 cup shredded or grated unsweetened dried coconut
- 1 scant pinch ground asafoetida
- 1 tablespoon coconut or peanut oil
- 1 tablespoon coriander seeds
- 1 tablespoon dried white split urad beans (dhulli urad dal), sorted
- 1 tablespoon dried yellow split chickpea (channa dal), sorted
- 1 teaspoon black mustard seeds
- 1 teaspoon cumin seeds
- 2 large cloves fresh garlic, crudely chopped
- 2 to 3 tablespoons Tamarind Paste
- 5 to 7 fresh curry leaves
- 7 dried red chile peppers, such as chile de arbol, 5 broken and 2 with stems

Directions:

1. Ready the tamarind paste. Next, preheat the oven to 250°F. Spread the coconut on a baking tray and roast until a golden colour is achieved, 20 to 30 minutes (depending on the moisture content).
2. In a small-sized non-stick saucepan, dry-roast together the broken red chile peppers, urad and channa dals, garlic, coriander, cumin, and fenugreek over moderate heat until seems slightly darker, approximately two minutes. Allow to cool, then grind using a spice or coffee grinder, in two batches if necessary, until a fine powder is achieved. Remove spices to a container. In the same grinder, grind the coconut, in two batches if necessary, to make it as fine as possible. Mix with the spices.
3. Heat the oil in a moderate-sized non-stick wok or saucepan using moderate to high heat and Put in the whole red chile peppers and mustard seeds; they should splutter upon contact with the hot oil, so reduce the heat and cover the pan until the spluttering diminishes. Put in the asafoetida and curry leaves, then stir in the coconut-spice mixture. Put in the tamarind paste and the salt,

and stir over moderate heat until well mixed. Move to a container and serve instantly, place in your fridge for approximately ten days, or freeze for no more than six months.

SEMOLINA-COCONUT CHUTNEY

This recipe is called "Sooji-kopra chutni" in Hindi

Yield: Approximately 1½ cups

Ingredients:

- ⅛ teaspoon ground asafoetida
- ⅓ cup fine-grain semolina
- ½ cup finely chopped fresh cilantro, including soft stems
- 1 cup non-fat plain yogurt
- 1 fresh green chile pepper, such as serrano, stemmed
- 1 tablespoon shredded or grated unsweetened dried coconut
- 1 teaspoon peanut oil
- 1 teaspoon salt, or to taste
- 15 to 20 fresh curry leaves
- 3 quarter-size slices of peeled fresh ginger

Directions:

1. Put the semolina and oil in a small-sized non-stick wok or saucepan and roast, stirring and swaying the pan using moderate to low heat, until the semolina is golden, approximately five minutes. Put in the coconut and asafoetida and cook, stirring, another two minutes.
2. Using a blender, mix together and pulse the yogurt, curry leaves, ginger, green chile pepper, and salt until the desired smoothness is achieved. Put in the roasted semolina and coconut mixture, and blend again until the desired smoothness is achieved. Allow to rest for approximately half an hour so the semolina can absorb the yogurt and expand. Move to a serving dish and refrigerate at least two hours. Stir in the cilantro and serve chilled. This chutney stays fresh in the fridge for approximately seven days. Do not freeze.

SHREDDED COCONUT CHUTNEY Ⓥ

This recipe is called "Kopra chutni" in Hindi

Yield: Approximately 1½ cups

Ingredients:

- ¼ to ⅓ cup water
- ½ cup crudely chopped fresh cilantro, including soft stems
- ½ teaspoon salt, or to taste
- ¾ cup fresh mint leaves
- 1¼ cups shredded or grated unsweetened dried coconut
- 2 fresh green chile peppers, such as serrano, stemmed
- 3 large cloves fresh garlic, peeled
- 3 to 4 tablespoons Tamarind Paste

Directions:

1. Ready the tamarind paste. Next, place the coconut in a medium size non-stick skillet and roast, stirring and swaying the pan over moderate heat until a golden colour is achieved, approximately two to three minutes.
2. Put all the rest of the ingredients using a blender or a food processor and process until a smooth purée is achieved. Stir in the roasted coconut and process once more until the desired smoothness is achieved. Move to a container and serve. This chutney stays fresh in the fridge for approximately ten days, or in the freezer about six months.

GARLIC AND CHILE PEPPER CHUTNEYS

GARLIC AND FRESH RED CHILE PEPPER CHUTNEY Ⓥ

This recipe is called "Lussan aur laal mirch ki chutni" in Hindi

Yield: Approximately 1½ cups

Ingredients:

- ¼ cup fresh lime juice, or to taste
- 1 tablespoon ground paprika
- 1 teaspoon cayenne pepper
- 1½ tablespoons ajwain seeds, crudely ground
- 15 to 20 fresh green chile peppers, such as serranos, crudely chopped
- 2 tablespoons black peppercorns, dry-roasted and ground (See the Dry Roasting section in Introduction)
- 2 to 3 red bell peppers, chopped
- 2 to 3 teaspoons salt, or to taste
- 6 to 8 large cloves fresh garlic, peeled
- 6 to 8 quarter-size slices of peeled fresh ginger

Directions:

1. Ready the peppercorns. Then place the garlic, ginger, red chile peppers, bell peppers, and lime juice Using a food processor or a blender and process until the desired smoothness is achieved. Put in the paprika, ajwain, 1½ tablespoons pepper, and the salt and process once more until the desired smoothness is achieved.

2. Move to a serving container, garnish with the rest of the pepper, and serve. This chutney stays fresh in the fridge for approximately thirty days or in the freezer about six months.

3. **Variation:** Make a simpler garlic chutney by processing together 2 large peeled heads fresh garlic, 2 teaspoons ground cayenne pepper, 1 small tomato, 1 teaspoon ground cumin seeds, and 1 teaspoon salt until a smooth paste is achieved.

GREEN GARLIC AND NUTS CHUTNEY Ⓥ

This recipe is called "Harae lussan aur nuts ki chutni" in Hindi

Yield: Approximately 1½ cups

Ingredients:

- ⅛ teaspoon ground asafoetida
- ¼ cup fresh lime or lemon juice, or to taste
- ¼ teaspoon ground paprika
- ½ cup fresh mint leaves
- ½ teaspoon black mustard seeds
- ½ teaspoon cumin seeds
- ½ teaspoon freshly ground black pepper, or to taste
- ¾ cup shelled and crudely chopped mixed raw nuts, such as walnuts, almonds, cashews, and pine nuts
- 1 tablespoon vegetable oil
- 1 teaspoon sugar
- 1½ cups crudely chopped fresh cilantro, including soft stems
- 1½ teaspoons salt, or to taste
- 3 to 5 fresh green chile peppers, such as serrano, stemmed
- 5 to 7 green garlic shoots (with bulbs), bottom 3 to 4 inches only, thinly chopped

Directions:

1. Using a food processor or a blender, combine and pulse the nuts, green chile peppers and garlic until minced. Put in the cilantro and mint to the work container and process, stopping intermittently to scrub the inner walls using a spatula, until puréed. While processing, trickle the lime juice through the feeder tube into the work container and pulse the chutney until the desired smoothness is achieved. Put in the sugar, salt, and black pepper and process once more. Tweak the seasonings to your taste. Move to a container.

2. Heat the oil in a big non-stick wok or saucepan using moderate to high heat and Put in the cumin and mustard seeds; they should splatter upon contact with the hot oil, so reduce the heat and cover the pan and reduce the heat until the splattering diminishes. Mix in the asafoetida and paprika just to blend, then move the spice mixture to the chutney and stir mildly to combine, with

parts of it visible as a decoration. Move to a container and serve instantly, place in your fridge for approximately ten days, or freeze for no more than six months.

PEANUT AND GARLIC CHUTNEY Ⓥ

This recipe is called "Moong-phalli aur lassun ki chutni" in Hindi

Yield: Approximately 1½ cups

Ingredients:

- ¼ cup <u>Tamarind Paste</u> or lemon juice
- ½ cup dried shredded unsweetened coconut
- ½ teaspoon salt, or to taste
- 1 tablespoon peanut oil
- 1 teaspoon black mustard seeds
- 1¼ cups roasted unsalted peanuts, without red skin
- 2 large cloves fresh garlic, peeled
- 4 to 5 dried red chile peppers, such as chiles de arbol, broken
- 5 to 7 fresh curry leaves

Directions:

1. Ready the tamarind paste. Next, in a small skillet, dry-roast the red chile peppers until seems slightly darker. Put the peppers Using a food processor or a blender. Put in the peanuts and process until fine. Then Put in the coconut, garlic, tamarind (or lemon juice), and salt, and pulse until a smooth and thick paste is achieved, adding up to ¼ cup water, as needed.
2. Move to a serving container. Heat the oil in a small saucepan using moderate to high heat. Put in the mustard seeds and curry leaves; they should splutter upon contact with the hot oil, so cover the pan until the spluttering diminishes. Swiftly put in the spice mixture to the chutney and stir mildly to combine, with parts of it visible as a decoration. Move to a container and serve instantly, place in your fridge for approximately ten days, or freeze for no more than six months.

BEAN AND LEGUME CHUTNEYS

CLASSIC HYDERABADI GINGER-SESAME CHUTNEY Ⓥ

This recipe is called "Hyderabad ki adrak-til chutni" in Hindi

Yield: Approximately 1½ cups

Ingredients:

- ⅛ teaspoon ground asafoetida
- ¼ cup Tamarind Paste, or to taste
- 1 cup peeled and crudely chopped fresh ginger
- 1 large clove fresh garlic, peeled
- 1 tablespoon white sesame seeds
- 1 teaspoon black mustard seeds
- 1 teaspoon cumin seeds
- 1 teaspoon salt, or to taste
- 1 to 3 fresh green chile peppers, such as serrano, chopped with seeds
- 2 dried red chile peppers, such as chile de arbol, broken
- 2 tablespoons grated jaggery (gur)
- 2 teaspoons Indian sesame oil
- 8 to 10 fresh curry leaves

Directions:

1. Ready the tamarind paste. Next, heat the oil in a small-sized non-stick saucepan using moderate to low heat and cook the ginger, stirring, until a golden colour is achieved, approximately five minutes. Using a slotted spoon, remove the fried ginger to a blender jar, leaving the oil behind in the pan.
2. In the same oil, put in the garlic and the green and red chile peppers and cook, stirring, until a golden colour is achieved. Tilt the pan to gather the oil to one side and Put in the cumin and mustard seeds; they should splutter upon contact with the hot oil, so reduce the heat and cover the pan until the

spluttering diminishes. Swiftly put in the curry leaves, sesame seeds, and asafoetida.

3. Move to the blender jar, put in the jaggery, tamarind paste, and the salt, and process until crudely puréed. Put in a tablespoon or 2 of hot water, if required, for blending. Move to a container and serve instantly, place in your fridge for approximately ten days, or freeze for no more than six months.

ROASTED BLACK CHICKPEA CHUTNEY WITH PEANUTS Ⓥ

This recipe is called "Kaalae channae ki chutni" in Hindi

Yield: Approximately 1½ cups

Ingredients:

- ¼ teaspoon salt, or to taste
- ½ cup crudely chopped fresh cilantro, including soft stems
- ½ cup dry-roasted unsalted peanuts, red skin removed
- ½ cup roasted black chickpeas (bhunae channae)
- ½ teaspoon sugar
- 1 to 2 fresh green chile peppers, such as serrano, stemmed
- 1 to 2 tablespoons fresh lime or lemon juice

Directions:

1. Rub off the black outer coating from the chickpeas (it comes off easily). Using a spice or coffee grinder, mix together and grind the chickpeas and peanuts until the desired smoothness is achieved.
2. Using a food processor or a blender, combine and pulse the cilantro, chile peppers, and lime juice, and then Put in the ground dal, peanuts, sugar, and salt. Process until well mixed. Move to a container and serve instantly, place in your fridge for approximately ten days, or freeze for no more than six months.

ROASTED DAL AND FRESH GREEN CHILE PEPPER CHUTNEY Ⓥ

This recipe is called "Bhel-puri ki chutni" in Hindi

Yield: Approximately 1½ cups

Ingredients:

- ¾ cup dried yellow split chickpeas (channa dal), sorted and washed in 3 to 4 changes of water
- 1½ teaspoons salt, or to taste
- 2 cups crudely chopped fresh cilantro, including soft stems
- 20 to 25 fresh green chile peppers, such as serrano, stemmed
- 3 to 4 tablespoons fresh lemon or lime juice
- 4 large cloves fresh garlic, peeled

Directions:

1. Put the dal in a small-sized cast-iron or non-stick skillet and dry-roast using moderate heat, stirring and swaying the pan until a golden colour is achieved, approximately a minute or two. Allow to cool, then grind using a spice or coffee grinder till you get a fine powder.
2. Put the cilantro, green chile peppers, garlic, and lemon juice using a blender or a food processor and process until the desired smoothness is achieved. Put in the ground dal and the salt and process once again to mix. Move to a container and serve instantly, place in your fridge for approximately ten days, or freeze for no more than six months.

SESAME-PEANUT CHUTNEY Ⓥ

This recipe is called "Til aur moong-phalli ki chutni" in Hindi

Yield: Approximately 1 cup

Ingredients:

- ¼ cup hot water
- ¼ cup white sesame seeds
- ½ cup crudely chopped fresh cilantro, including soft stems
- ½ cup dry-roasted unsalted peanuts, red skins removed
- ½ cup Tamarind Paste
- 1 large clove fresh garlic, peeled
- 1 teaspoon salt, or to taste
- 1 to 3 fresh green chile peppers, such as serrano, stemmed

Directions:

1. Ready the tamarind paste. Next, in a small skillet, roast the sesame seeds over moderate heat, stirring and swaying the pan until a golden colour is achieved, approximately one minute. Move to a blender along with all the other ingredients and pulse until the desired smoothness is achieved.
2. Tweak the seasonings to your taste. Move to a container and serve instantly, place in your fridge for approximately ten days, or freeze for no more than six months.

YOGURT CHUTNEYS

YOGURT CHEESE CHUTNEY WITH MINCED GREENS

This recipe is called "Gaadhi dahi ki hari chutni" in Hindi

Yield: Approximately 1½ cups

Ingredients:

- ¼ cup minced fresh cilantro, including soft stems
- ¼ cup minced fresh mint leaves
- ¼ teaspoon ground paprika

- 1 (2-foot-square) piece of fine muslin or 4 layers of cheesecloth
- 1 fresh green chile pepper, such as serrano, minced with seeds
- 1 tablespoon peeled and minced fresh ginger
- 1 teaspoon Chaat Masala, or to taste (Homemade or store-bought)
- 1 teaspoon dry-roasted and crudely crushed cumin seeds (See the dry-roasting section in Introduction)
- 10 to 12 scallions, white parts only, minced
- 1½ cups non-fat plain yogurt
- 2 tablespoons fresh lemon juice

Directions:

1. Ready the cumin and the chaat masala. Next, place the yogurt in a colander or a fine-mesh strainer lined with muslin or 4 layers of cheesecloth set over a container. let drain about two hours in a fridge. Move to a serving container, then whisk with a fork until the desired smoothness is achieved.

2. Put in the scallion, cilantro, mint, ginger, green chile pepper, lemon juice, chaat masala, sugar, and half the cumin, and mix thoroughly. Tweak the seasonings to your taste. Garnish with the rest of the cumin seeds and the paprika, and serve instantly or place in your fridge for approximately seven days. Do not freeze.

YOGURT CHUTNEY WITH PURÉED GREENS

This recipe is called "Dahi ki hari chutni" in Hindi

Yield: Approximately 1½ cups

Ingredients:

- ½ teaspoon crudely ground black pepper
- 1 cup non-fat plain yogurt, whisked until the desired smoothness is achieved
- 1 teaspoon Chaat Masala, or to taste (Homemade or store-bought)
- 1 teaspoon salt, or to taste
- 1 to 3 fresh green chile peppers, such as serrano, stemmed

- 2 cups crudely chopped mixed fresh herbs in any proportion, such as cilantro, mint, parsley, dill, basil, or lemon basil
- 2 tablespoons fresh lime or lemon juice
- 4 quarter-size slices of peeled fresh ginger
- 5 to 6 scallions, crudely chopped
- Minced fresh greens of your choice (scallions, chile peppers, or herbs)

Directions:

1. Ready the chaat masala. Next, Using a food processor or a blender, combine and pulse the ginger, scallions, and green chile peppers until minced. Put in the fresh herbs and lime juice and process once more until the desired smoothness is achieved, scraping the sides of the work container using a spatula, as required. (If you need more liquid while processing, stir in some of the yogurt.) Put in the chaat masala, salt, and pepper, and process once more.
2. Put the yogurt in a serving container and Put in the puréed greens. Swirl lightly to combine, with parts of the greens visible as a decoration. Scatter the additional minced greens on top, and serve. This chutney stays fresh in the fridge for approximately seven days. Do not freeze.

YOGURT CHUTNEY WITH ROASTED DALS AND SPICES

This recipe is called "Dahi aur bhuni dal ki chutni" in Hindi

Yield: Approximately 1½ cups

Ingredients:

- ¼ cup grated fresh or frozen coconut
- ¼ teaspoon ground asafoetida
- ½ cup crudely chopped fresh cilantro, including soft stems
- 1 cup non-fat plain yogurt, whisked until the desired smoothness is achieved
- 1 tablespoon each, dried yellow split chickpeas (channa dal), split white urad beans (dhulli urad dal), yellow mung beans (dhulli mung dal), dry-roasted and ground (See the dry-roasting section in Introduction)
- 1 tablespoon vegetable oil

- 1 teaspoon black mustard seeds
- 1 teaspoon salt, or to taste
- 1 to 2 fresh green chile peppers, such as serrano, crudely chopped
- 15 to 20 fresh curry leaves
- 2 dried red chile peppers, such as chile de arbol, with stems, broken
- 2 tablespoons peeled and crudely chopped fresh ginger
- 2 teaspoons cumin seeds, dry-roasted and crudely ground (See the dry-roasting section in Introduction)

Directions:

1. Ready the dals and the cumin. Then heat the oil in a small-sized non-stick wok or saucepan using moderate to high heat and Put in the red chile peppers and mustard seeds; they should splutter upon contact with the hot oil, so reduce the heat and cover the pan until the spluttering diminishes.
2. Swiftly put in the asafoetida, curry leaves, green chile peppers, coconut, and ginger, and cook, stirring, until the coconut is golden, approximately five minutes. Put in the cilantro and stir another 5 minutes. Move to a blender or a food processor and process until a smooth paste is achieved.
3. Put the yogurt in a serving container, stir in the processed herb and coconut paste, then Put in the roasted dals, cumin (save some cumin for garnish), and the salt, and stir to mix thoroughly. Sprinkle the reserved cumin on top and serve. This chutney stays fresh in the fridge for approximately seven days. Do not freeze.

YOGURT-ALMOND CHUTNEY

This recipe is called "Dahi-badaam ki chutni" in Hindi

Yield: Approximately 1½ cups

Ingredients:

- ¼ cup minced fresh cilantro, including soft stems
- ½ cup shelled and crudely ground raw almonds
- 1 cup non-fat plain yogurt, whisked until the desired smoothness is achieved
- 1 fresh green chile pepper, such as serrano, minced with seeds
- 1 tablespoon fresh lemon juice

- 1 tablespoon peeled and minced fresh ginger
- 1 teaspoon <u>Chaat Masala</u> (Homemade or store-bought)
- 1 teaspoon salt, or to taste
- Freshly ground black pepper, to taste

Directions:

1. In a serving container, combine all the ingredients except the chaat masala and chill at least 4 hours.
2. Before serving, ready the chaat masala then add it to the chutney and stir mildly to combine, with parts of it visible as a decoration. This chutney stays fresh about seven days in a fridge. Do not freeze.

PURÉED FRUIT CHUTNEYS

PURÉED FRESH MANGO-GINGER CHUTNEY Ⓥ

This recipe is called "Pakkae aam ki chutni" in Hindi

Yield: Approximately 1½ cups

Ingredients:

- ¼ cup finely chopped fresh cilantro, including soft stems
- ¼ cup fresh lime or lemon juice
- ½ teaspoon salt, or to taste
- 1 to 2 fresh green chile pepper, such as serrano, minced with seeds
- 2 tablespoons peeled and minced fresh ginger
- 3 large ripe mangoes (about ¾ pound each), washed and wiped dry
- Freshly ground black pepper

Directions:

1. Using a knife, peel the mango, then crudely cut the fruit around the center seed. Put the mango pieces in a big serving container and mash with a fork to make the fruit as smooth as possible.
2. Stir in all the rest of the ingredients. Garnish with black pepper and serve instantly, or place in your fridge for a maximum of seven days.

PURÉED GREEN MANGO CHUTNEY Ⓥ

This recipe is called "Harae aam ki chutni" in Hindi

Yield: Approximately 1½ cups

Ingredients:

- ⅛ teaspoon ground asafoetida
- ½ teaspoon crudely ground fenugreek seeds
- ½ teaspoon salt, or to taste
- 1 tablespoon peanut oil
- 1 teaspoon black mustard seeds
- 1 to 2 teaspoons sugar (not compulsory)
- 1 to 3 fresh green chile peppers, such as serrano, stemmed
- 15 to 20 fresh curry leaves
- 2 large unripe green mangoes (about ¾ pound each), washed and wiped dry
- 2 whole dried red chile peppers, such as chile de arbol
- 3 quarter-size slices peeled fresh ginger
- 4 scallions, crudely chopped

Directions:

1. Using a vegetable peeler, peel the mangoes, then cut the fruit around the center seed into ½- to 1-inch pieces. Put the mango pieces and the ginger, green chile peppers, scallions, curry leaves, and salt Using a food processor or a blender, and process until minced. Transfer to a serving container. Add some of the sugar if the chutney appears too tart.
2. Heat the oil in a small-sized non-stick saucepan using moderate to high heat and Put in the red chile peppers and mustard seeds; they should splutter upon contact with the hot oil, so reduce the heat and cover the pan until the spluttering diminishes. Swiftly put in the fenugreek seeds and asafoetida, stir

for about half a minute, then add this seasoning mixture to the chutney, with parts of it visible as a decoration. Move to a container and serve instantly, place in your fridge for approximately ten days, or freeze for no more than six months.

SOUTH INDIAN TOMATO CHUTNEY Ⓥ

This recipe is called "South ki tamatar chutni" in Hindi

Yield: Approximately 1½ cups

Ingredients:

- ¼ cup peanut oil
- ½ cup finely chopped red onion
- ½ teaspoon black peppercorns
- 1 (15-ounce) can tomato sauce
- 1 tablespoon coriander seeds
- 1 teaspoon black mustard seeds
- 1 teaspoon cayenne pepper, or to taste
- 1 teaspoon cumin seeds
- 1 teaspoon dried curry leaves
- 1 teaspoon dried white urad beans (dhulli urad dal), sorted
- 1 teaspoon dried yellow split chickpeas (channa dal), sorted
- 1 teaspoon salt, or to taste
- 1 teaspoon Tamarind Paste
- 2 large cloves fresh garlic, minced
- 2 to 3 whole dried red chile peppers, such as chile de arbol

Directions:

1. Ready the tamarind paste. Next, in a spice or a coffee grinder, mix together and grind coriander and cumin seeds, dals, and peppercorns until a fine powder is achieved.
2. Heat the oil in a small-sized non-stick saucepan over moderate heat and Put in the mustard seeds, curry leaves, and red chile peppers; they should splutter upon contact with the hot oil, so reduce the heat and cover the pan until the spluttering diminishes. Swiftly put in the garlic and onion, stir a few seconds,

then Put in the ground spice and dal mixture, cayenne pepper, and salt and cook, stirring, another two minutes.

3. Put in the tomato sauce and tamarind paste, cover the pan, reduce the heat to low, and cook, stirring intermittently, until the chutney is thick and fragrant and reduced to about 1 cup, approximately twenty minutes. Allow to cool, then serve instantly, place in your fridge for approximately sixty days or freeze about six months.

TART APPLE-GINGER CHUTNEY Ⓥ

This recipe is called "Saeb, adrak aur harae tamatar ki chutni" in Hindi

Yield: Approximately 2 cups

Ingredients:

- 1 tablespoon coriander seeds
- 1 tablespoon peanut oil
- 1 teaspoon black peppercorns, dry-roasted and crudely ground (See the Dry Roasting section in Introduction)
- 1 teaspoon salt, or to taste
- 1 teaspoon sugar
- 2 fresh green chile peppers, such as serrano, stemmed
- 2 large tart green apples, such as Granny Smith or pippin, cored and crudely chopped
- 2 small green tomatoes, crudely chopped
- 6 to 8 quarter-size slices of peeled fresh ginger
- Fresh cilantro sprigs

Directions:

1. Ready the peppercorns. Then heat the oil in a small saucepan using moderate to high heat and Put in the coriander seeds; they should sizzle upon contact with the hot oil. Swiftly put in the rest of the ingredients and cook, stirring, approximately five minutes.

2. Move to a food processor or a blender and process to make a coarse purée. Move to a container, garnish with cilantro sprigs, and serve. This chutney stays

fresh in the fridge for approximately ten days, and in the freezer about six months.

PRESERVED CHUTNEYS

CRANBERRY CHUTNEY PRESERVE Ⓥ

This recipe is called "Karonda chutni" in Hindi

Yield: Approximately 4 cups

Ingredients:

- 1 tablespoon ground ginger
- 1 tablespoon vegetable oil
- 10 to 12 whole cloves
- 1½ teaspoons salt, or to taste
- 2 (12-ounce) packages fresh cranberries, washed
- 2 (1-inch) sticks cinnamon
- 2 tablespoons Bengali 5-Spices (Panch-Phoran), crudely ground
- 2 tablespoons peeled and minced fresh ginger
- 4 cups sugar
- 4 cups water
- 5 to 7 tablespoons distilled white vinegar
- 8 to 10 black cardamom pods, crushed lightly to break the skin

Directions:

1. Ready the 5-spices. Next, heat the oil in a big non-reactive wok or saucepan using moderate to high heat and cook the cinnamon, cardamom pods, and cloves, stirring, approximately half a minute.
2. Put in the fresh ginger and panch-phoran and cook, stirring, approximately one minute. Put in the cranberries, sugar, water, ground ginger, and salt, and bring

to a boil using high heat. Cover and cook, stirring intermittently, until slightly thickened, approximately 7 minutes.

3. Reduce the heat to medium, uncover the pan, put in the vinegar, and cook until the chutney is quite thick, approximately ten minutes. (Do not make the chutney very thick; it will thicken as it cools.) Move to a container, allow to cool down, and serve at room temperature, or refrigerate at least two hours and serve chilled. This chutney stays fresh in the fridge for approximately three months, or in the freezer about 1 year.

FRAGRANT MANGO CHUTNEY PRESERVE Ⓥ

This recipe is called "Aam ki chutni" in Hindi

Yield: Approximately 4 cups

Ingredients:

- ¾ cup distilled white vinegar
- 1 tablespoon black peppercorns
- 1 tablespoon fennel seeds
- 1 tablespoon fenugreek seeds
- 1 tablespoon salt, or to taste
- 1 tablespoon whole cloves
- 10 to 12 black cardamom pods, crushed lightly to break the skin
- 10 to 12 green cardamom pods, crushed lightly to break the skin
- 1½ teaspoons kalonji seeds
- 2 (3-inch) sticks cinnamon, broken
- 4 cups sugar
- 4 large unripe green mangoes, (about ¾ pound each), washed and wiped dry

Directions:

1. Using a vegetable peeler, peel the mangoes, then cut the fruit around the center seed into thin 1½- to 2-inch long pieces. Put all the spices in a large, heavy, non-reactive saucepan and roast using moderate to high heat, stirring and swaying the pan, until heated through, approximately one minute.

2. Put in the mangoes, sugar, and salt, and bring to a boil, stirring continuously using moderate to high heat until the sugar melts and comes to a boil. Boil 1 minute, then reduce the heat to medium-low, cover the pan and cook, stirring intermittently, approximately ten minutes.
3. Uncover the pan, put in the vinegar, and cook, stirring intermittently, until the sugar caramelizes and takes on a rich honey-like color and consistency, approximately twenty minutes. (Do not make the chutney very thick; it will thicken as it cools.)
4. Allow to cool completely, then put it in sterile jars. This chutney does not need to be refrigerated. It stays fresh about six months at room temperature. The color deepens over time, but that does not affect the taste.

RED TOMATO CHUTNEY PRESERVE Ⓥ

This recipe is called "Tamatar-til ki chutni" in Hindi

Yield: Approximately 2 cups

Ingredients:

- ⅛ teaspoon ground asafoetida
- ¼ teaspoon ground turmeric
- 1 cup finely chopped onion
- 1 tablespoon black mustard seeds
- 1 tablespoon dried split pigeon peas (toor dal), sorted
- 1 tablespoon dried yellow split chickpeas (channa dal), sorted
- 1 tablespoon minced fresh garlic cloves
- 1 tablespoon sesame seeds, dry-roasted (See the dry-roasting section in Introduction)
- 1 teaspoon salt, or to taste
- 1 to 3 fresh green chile peppers, such as serrano, minced with seeds
- 2 large tomatoes, finely chopped
- 2 tablespoons distilled white vinegar
- 2 tablespoons minced fresh curry leaves
- 2 tablespoons peanut oil
- 2 tablespoons peeled and minced fresh ginger

Directions:

1. Ready the sesame seeds. Next, heat the oil in a medium wok or saucepan using moderate to high heat and Put in the mustard seeds; they should splutter upon contact with the hot oil, so reduce the heat and cover the pan until the spluttering diminishes. Put in the curry leaves and both the dals, and stir until the dals are golden, approximately half a minute. Put in the onion and cook, stirring, until a golden colour is achieved, approximately three minutes. Put in the ginger, garlic, and green chile peppers, stir 1 minute, then stir in the turmeric, salt, and asafoetida.

2. Put in the tomatoes and vinegar and cook until most of the fluids vaporize and the chutney is semi-thick, approximately eight to ten minutes. (It will continue to thicken as it cools.) Move to a serving dish, garnish with the sesame seeds, and serve hot or cold, or store in an airtight vessel in the refrigerator, approximately 1 year.

SPICY APPLE-GINGER CHUTNEY PRESERVE Ⓥ

This recipe is called "Saeb-adrak ki chutni" in Hindi

Yield: Approximately 4 cups

Ingredients:

- ¼ cup distilled white vinegar
- 10 whole cloves
- 1½ tablespoons salt
- 2 cups sugar
- 2 medium onions, cut in half along the length and thinly chopped
- 2 pounds tart apples, such as Pippin or Granny Smith, peeled and cut in ½-inch pieces
- 2 tablespoons Basic Ginger-Garlic Paste (Homemade or store-bought)
- 2 tablespoons fennel seeds
- 2 teaspoons crudely ground fenugreek seeds
- 2 teaspoons kalonji seeds
- 2 to 3 teaspoons cayenne pepper

- 20 to 25 dried red chile peppers, such as chile de arbol, with stems
- 3 tablespoons vegetable oil
- 4 (1-inch) sticks cinnamon
- 5 to 6 (1-inch) pieces peeled fresh ginger, cut in half along the length and thinly chopped
- 6 fresh garlic cloves, cut in half along the length and thinly chopped
- 6 to 8 black cardamom pods, crushed lightly to break the skin

Directions:

1. Ready the ginger-garlic paste. Next, heat the oil in a big non-stick wok or saucepan using moderate to high heat and cook the red chile peppers, cinnamon, cardamom pods, and cloves, stirring, approximately one minute. Put in the fennel and kalonji seeds, and stir for approximately half a minute, then Put in the onion, ginger, and garlic and cook, stirring until a golden colour is achieved, approximately ten minutes.
2. Put in the fenugreek seeds and cayenne pepper and stir 1 minute. Then Put in the apples, sugar, ginger-garlic paste, and salt, and cook over moderate heat, stirring, until the sugar melts, approximately three minutes. Increase the heat to medium-high and cook until the sugar caramelizes into a rich golden color, the apples are soft, and the chutney is thick, approximately fifteen minutes.
3. Put in the vinegar and boil using high heat approximately two minutes, or until the chutney thickens once more. (Do not make the chutney very thick; it will thicken as it cools.) Allow to cool completely and put in sterile jars. This chutney does not need to be refrigerated. It stays fresh about six months at room temperature. The color deepens over time, but that does not affect the taste.

SPICY APRICOT CHUTNEY PRESERVE Ⓥ

This recipe is called "Aadu ki chutni" in Hindi

Yield: Approximately 4 cups

Ingredients:

- ¼ cup Basic Ginger-Garlic Paste (Homemade or store-bought)
- ¼ to ⅓ cup distilled white vinegar

- ¾ teaspoon ground fenugreek seeds
- 1 tablespoon ground fennel seeds
- 1 teaspoon kalonji seeds
- 1½ cups sugar
- 2 pounds fresh unripe apricots, pitted and cut into wedges
- 2 tablespoons salt, or to taste
- 3 (1-inch) sticks cinnamon
- 3 small onions, cut in half along the length and thinly chopped
- 3 tablespoons vegetable oil
- 5 to 7 fresh green chile peppers, such as serrano, minced with seeds
- 6 to 8 black cardamom pods, crushed lightly to break the skin
- 8 whole cloves

Directions:

1. Ready the ginger-garlic paste. Next, heat the oil in a big non-stick wok or saucepan using moderate to high heat and cook the cinnamon, cardamom pods, and cloves, stirring, approximately one minute. Put in the onions and cook, stirring, until a golden colour is achieved, approximately 7 minutes. Put in the kalonji, fenugreek, and fennel seeds, and then stir in the ginger-garlic paste and green chile peppers and sauté approximately two minutes.
2. Put in the apricots, sugar, and salt and cook, stir-ring, over moderate heat until the sugar melts, approximately three minutes. Increase the heat to medium-high and cook until the sugar caramelizes into a rich golden color, the apricots are soft, and the chutney is thick, approximately fifteen minutes.
3. Put in the vinegar, and boil using high heat approximately two minutes, or until the chutney thickens once more. (Do not make the chutney very thick; it will thicken as it cools.) Allow to cool completely, and put in sterile jars. This chutney does not need to be refrigerated. It stays fresh about six months at room temperature. The color deepens over time, but that does not affect the taste.

TOMATO CHUTNEY PRESERVE Ⓥ

This recipe is called "Tamatar, kaaju aur kishmish ki chutni" in Hindi

Yield: Approximately 2 cups

Ingredients:

- ½ cup crudely chopped raw cashews
- ½ cup distilled white vinegar
- ½ cup golden raisins
- ½ teaspoon crudely crushed fenugreek seeds
- ½ teaspoon cayenne pepper
- 1 tablespoon salt, or to taste
- 1 tablespoon vegetable oil
- 1 teaspoon fennel seeds
- 1 teaspoon ground paprika
- 2 cups sugar, or more to taste
- 2 large fresh garlic cloves, minced
- 2 tablespoons peeled and minced fresh ginger
- 2 to 4 fresh green chile peppers, minced with seeds
- 3 large tomatoes, finely chopped (about 1½ pounds)

Directions:

1. Heat the oil in a big non-reactive wok or saucepan over moderate heat and cook the ginger, garlic, green chile peppers, fennel seeds and fenugreek seeds, stirring, until a golden colour is achieved, approximately one minute. Put in the cashews and raisins and stir until the raisins expand, approximately one minute.

2. Put in the tomatoes, sugar, salt, paprika, and cayenne pepper and cook, using moderate to high heat for the first two to three minutes. Then cover the pan and cook, stirring intermittently, over moderate heat until the tomatoes are very soft, approximately ten minutes. Put in the vinegar, and simmer, uncovered, until semi-thick, approximately fifteen minutes. (It will continue to thicken as it cools.) Serve instantly or allow to cool down, then store in an airtight vessel in the refrigerator, approximately 1 year.

SONTH CHUTNEYS

These are delicious sweet and sour chutneys commonly seen in Indian restaurants.

MINTY SONTH CHUTNEY WITH MANGO

Ⓥ

This recipe is called "Pudina sonth" in Hindi

Yield: Approximately 4 cups

Ingredients:

- ½ teaspoon black salt
- ½ teaspoon ground ginger
- 1 cup crudely grated or crushed jaggery, or 1¼ cup dark brown sugar
- 1 cup mango or tamarind powder, sifted to remove any lumps
- 1 teaspoon ground paprika
- 1 to 3 fresh green chile peppers, such as serrano, stemmed
- 1½ tablespoons cumin seeds, dry-roasted and crudely ground (See the dry-roasting section in Introduction)
- 2 tablespoons Chaat Masala (Homemade or store-bought)
- 2 teaspoon salt, or to taste
- 20 to 25 large fresh mint leaves
- 3 to 4 cups water
- 8 quarter-size slices of peeled fresh ginger

Directions:

1. Ready the cumin seeds and chaat masala. Next, in a blender, mix together and pulse the ginger, chile peppers, mint leaves with about ½ cup of the water until a smooth paste is achieved.

2. In a large non-reactive saucepan, combine the jaggery and 3 cups of the water (disregard any lumps; they will melt when heated) and bring to a boil, stirring intermittently, until all the lumps dissolve completely, about three to four minutes. Pass through a fine-mesh strainer to filter out any impurities. Put the jaggery back into the saucepan and Put in the ginger-mint mixture, mango or tamarind powder, chaat masala, paprika, ground ginger, cumin, salt, and black salt.

3. Bring to a boil using high heat. Reduce the heat to moderate to low, and simmer, stirring intermittently, approximately five minutes. The sauce should be like a semi-thick batter. Stir in up to 1 cup of water if the sauce becomes

thick too swiftly. Adjust seasoning, move to a container, then allow to cool down. Serve at room temperature. Or move to an airtight vessel and place in your fridge for approximately sixty days, or freeze about 1 year.

SONTH CHUTNEY WITH DRIED MANGO SLICES Ⓥ Ⓟ

This recipe is called "Amchur ki sonth" in Hindi

Yield: Approximately 4 cups

Ingredients:

- 1 (2-inch) piece dried ginger, crudely chopped
- 1 cup crudely grated or crushed jaggery, or 1¼ cups dark brown sugar
- 1 tablespoon <u>Chaat Masala</u>, or to taste (Homemade or store-bought)
- 1 tablespoon cumin seeds, dry-roasted and finely ground (See the dry-roasting section in Introduction)
- 1 teaspoon black salt
- 1 teaspoon ground paprika
- 2 teaspoons salt, or to taste
- 4 cups water
- 4 ounces dried raw mango slices
- 4 to 6 dried red chile peppers, such as chile de arbol, broken

Directions:

1. Ready the cumin seeds and chaat masala. Next, place everything (except 1 cup of the water) into your pressure cooker. Ensure that the lid is secure, and cook using high heat until the regulator shows that the pressure is high, then cook for approximately a minute more. Take the pot off the heat or turn off the heat and let the pressure release automatically, twelve to fifteen minutes. Cautiously take the lid off.
2. Pass everything through a food mill into a big container to extract a smooth sauce. Bring the reserved one cup of water to a boil in a small saucepan. Pour the boiling hot water over the fibrous residue in the food mill and collect the rest of the pulp. Mix the extra pulp into the sauce; it should be like a semi-thick

batter. Tweak the seasonings to your taste, move to a container and serve at room temperature, or move to an airtight vessel and place in your fridge for approximately sixty days, or freeze about 1 year.

SONTH CHUTNEY WITH FRESH AND DRIED FRUITS Ⓥ

This recipe is called "Fallon vaali sonth" in Hindi

Yield: Approximately 4 cups

Ingredients:

- 1 cup crudely grated or crushed jaggery, or 1¼ cups dark brown sugar
- 1 cup finely chopped mixed dried fruits, such as raisins, peaches, apricots, plums, figs, and dates
- 1 cup mango or tamarind powder, sifted to remove lumps
- 1 tablespoon peeled and finely minced fresh ginger
- 1 tablespoon vegetable oil
- 1 teaspoon black salt
- 1 teaspoon cumin seeds
- 1 teaspoon ground paprika
- 1 to 2 cups chopped ripe fruits, such as bananas, mangoes, pineapple, and peaches
- 1½ cups water + 4 cups water, measured separately
- 2 tablespoons Chaat Masala, or to taste (Homemade or store-bought)
- 2 tablespoons cumin seeds, dry-roasted and ground (See the dry-roasting section in Introduction)
- 2 teaspoons ground ginger
- 2 teaspoons salt, or to taste

Directions:

1. Immerse the dried fruits overnight in 1½ cups of the water. In the meantime, ready the cumin seeds and chaat masala. When ready, drain the fruits, reserving the water.

2. In a large non-reactive saucepan, combine the jaggery and 2 cups of the water (disregard any lumps; they will melt when heated), and bring to a boil using high heat, stirring intermittently, until all the lumps dissolve completely, about three to four minutes. Pass through a fine-mesh strainer to filter out any impurities. Return to the pan. Stir in the mango or tamarind powder and up to 2 cups water, including the reserved fruit-water in this measurement. Mix thoroughly and bring to a boil using high heat.

3. Put in the drained dried fruits, fresh and dried ginger, chaat masala, salt, and black salt, reduce the heat to moderate to low, and simmer, stirring intermittently and pouring in additional water if the sauce becomes thick too swiftly, until it reaches a semi-thick batter-like consistency, approximately ten minutes. Tweak the seasonings to your taste and move to a serving container.

4. Heat the oil in a big non-stick wok or saucepan using moderate to high heat and Put in the cumin seeds; they should sizzle upon contact with the hot oil. Swiftly, take the pan off the heat, put in the paprika, and Combine with the chutney. Serve at room temperature, or move to an airtight vessel and place in your fridge for approximately sixty days, or freeze for approximately a year. Just before serving, stir in ripe fruits and serve.

SWEET SONTH CHUTNEY WITH DATES

Ⓥ

This recipe is called "Khajjur ki sonth" in Hindi

Yield: Approximately 4 cups

Ingredients:

- ½ cup seedless tamarind pulp
- ½ to ¾ cup sugar
- 1 teaspoon salt, or to taste
- 1½ tablespoons cumin seeds, dry-roasted and crudely ground (See the dry-roasting section in Introduction)
- 2 cups chopped pitted dates
- 2 cups hot water

Directions:

1. Ready the cumin seeds. Immerse the dates and tamarind pulp in 1 cup hot water, approximately one hour to soften.
2. Using your sanitized fingers, mush the pulp to separate it from the fibrous parts of the dates and to separate any tamarind seeds that may still be present. Next, pass the softened date-tamarind pulp through a fine-mesh strainer or a food mill into a big container to extract a smooth paste. Pour the rest of the hot water over the fibrous residue in the food mill and collect the rest of the pulp and Combine with the already extracted paste.
3. Move to a small saucepan, put in the sugar, cumin, and salt, and bring to a boil using high heat. Reduce the heat to moderate to low and simmer approximately five minutes. Stir in up to 1 cup of water if the chutney becomes thick too swiftly. Adjust the seasoning, then allow to cool down. Serve at room temperature, or move to an airtight vessel and place in your fridge for approximately sixty days, or freeze about a year.

INDIAN PICKLES

Pickles are highly popular in India. Most of the Indian households make their own pickles at home, and in bulk to last a year. Mango, lemon, and green chiles are three of the most popular pickle ingredients. Indian pickles have a long shelf life, and a few of the pickles can even last for a decade!

MANGO PICKLES

Mango pickles are the most common pickles you will find in India. It is virtually impossible to find a household where there is no mango pickle.

QUICK MANGO PICKLE Ⓥ

This recipe is called "Aam ka achaar" in Hindi

Yield: Approximately 2 cups

The mangoes are peeled for this recipe to hasten the process.

Ingredients:

- ⅛ teaspoon ground asafoetida
- 1 cup mustard or olive oil
- 1 tablespoon salt, or to taste
- 1 teaspoon black peppercorns, crudely ground
- 1 teaspoon ground turmeric
- 2 large unripe green mangoes (about ¾ pound each), washed and wiped dry
- 2 tablespoons Bengali Five Whole Spice Blend (Panch-Phoran), crudely ground (see basic spice blends section to create your own, or buy from a store)
- 3 large cloves fresh garlic, crudely chopped

Directions:

1. Ready the 5-spices. Next, using a vegetable peeler, peel the mango, then cut the fruit around the center seed into thin ½-inch-by-2-inch pieces. Heat the oil in a big non-stick wok or saucepan using moderate to high heat and put in the garlic, panch-phoran, peppercorns, turmeric, and asafoetida. They should sizzle when they touch the hot oil.
2. Swiftly put in the mangoes and the salt, decrease the heat to medium and cook, stirring, until the mangoes absorb all the flavours, fifteen to twenty minutes. Allow to cool and let marinate at room temperature for minimum two days before you serve. Store in the fridge for approximately one month. Serve chilled or at room temperature.

PUNJABI MANGO PICKLE Ⓥ

This recipe is called "Punjabi aam ka achaar" in Hindi

Yield: Approximately 6 cups

A classic mango pickle from my hometown!

Ingredients:

- ¼ cup fenugreek seeds
- ½ cup fennel seeds
- ½ cup salt, or to taste
- 1 small piece of muslin or 4 layers of cheesecloth (sufficient to cover the mouth of the jar)
- 1½ to 2 cups mustard oil or olive oil
- 2 tablespoons black peppercorns
- 2 tablespoons kalonji seeds
- 2 teaspoons cayenne pepper, or to taste
- 2 teaspoons ground turmeric
- 4 large unripe green mangoes (about ¾ pound each), washed and wiped dry

Directions:

1. Cut each unpeeled mango around the center seed into 1-inch-by-½-inch pieces. Throw away the center seeds. Using a spice or coffee grinder, very crudely mix together and grind all the whole spices. Move to a container and stir in the salt, turmeric, and cayenne pepper.
2. Heat the oil in a big non-stick wok or saucepan using moderate to high heat until just smoking, and put in the spice mixture. It should sizzle when it touches the hot oil. Turn off the heat and stir, approximately half a minute. Put in the mangoes and mix thoroughly, making sure all the pieces are thoroughly coated with the spices.
3. Allow to cool and move to a big sanitized glass jar. Make sure there is minimum ½ inch of oil on the surface. (Heat and add more oil, if required.) Cover the jar with the muslin, locking it using a rubber band, and if there is a warm sunny spot in the kitchen, put it there, else put it outdoors where there it can get some sun, swaying the jar a couple of times per day until the spices are plump and soft and the mango pieces are crisp-tender, about ten to twelve days. (bring the jar indoors in the evening if you're keeping it outdoors.) This pickle can be stored safely at room temperature for approximately two years.

MANGO PICKLE SPICE ROAST Ⓥ

This recipe is called "Bhuna Masala aam ka achaar" in Hindi

Yield: Approximately 6 cups

Basically the same recipe as the Punjabi mango pickle, with an added punch of roasted spices!

Ingredients:

- ¼ cup fenugreek seeds
- ½ cup salt
- ⅔ cup fennel seeds
- 1 small piece of muslin or 4 layers of cheesecloth (sufficient to cover the mouth of the jar)
- 1½ cups mustard or olive oil
- 2 tablespoons black peppercorns
- 2 tablespoons kalonji seeds
- 2 teaspoons cayenne pepper, or to taste
- 2 teaspoons ground paprika
- 2 teaspoons ground turmeric
- 4 large unripe green mangoes (about ¾ pound each), washed and wiped dry

Directions:

1. Cut each unpeeled mango around the center seed into 1-inch-by-½-inch pieces. Throw away the center seeds.
2. Put the fennel, fenugreek, kalonji, and peppercorns in a heavy cast-iron skillet and dry-roast the spices, stirring and swaying the pan over moderate heat, until slightly darker and fragrant, approximately three minutes. Allow to cool and move to a spice or coffee grinder, and grind crudely. Move to a container and stir in the salt, turmeric, paprika, and cayenne pepper.
3. Heat the oil in a moderate-sized non-stick wok or saucepan using moderate to high heat until just smoking. Allow to cool until just lukewarm, then Put in the spice mixture and the mangoes and mix thoroughly, ensuring all the pieces are thoroughly coated with the spices.
4. Move to a big sanitized glass jar. Make sure there is minimum ½ inch of oil on the surface. Cover the jar with the muslin, locking it using a rubber band, and if there is a warm sunny spot in the kitchen, put it there, else put it outdoors where there it can get some sun, swaying the jar a couple of times per day until the spices are plump and soft and the mango pieces are crisp-tender, about ten to twelve days. (bring the jar indoors in the evening if you're keeping it outdoors.) This pickle can be stored safely at room temperature for approximately two years.

COOKED SOUTH INDIAN MANGO PICKLE

This recipe is called "Dakshini aam ka achaar" in Hindi

Yield: Approximately 2 cups

As the name suggests, this pickle is cooked, and not sun-cured like the others.

Ingredients:

- ¼ teaspoon ground asafoetida
- ⅓ cup mustard or peanut oil
- ½ teaspoon ground turmeric
- 2 large unripe green mangoes (about ¾ pound each), washed and wiped dry
- 2 tablespoons salt
- 2 teaspoons black mustard seeds, crudely ground
- 2 teaspoons fenugreek seeds
- 3 to 5 dried red chile peppers, such as chile de arbol, broken

Directions:

1. Cut each unpeeled mango around the center seed into 1-inch-by-½-inch pieces. Throw away the center seeds. Put the mango in a container, put in the turmeric, and toss to mix thoroughly.
2. In a small skillet, roast the red chile peppers and fenugreek seeds over moderate heat until a golden colour is achieved, approximately one minute. Allow to cool and grind using a spice or coffee grinder till you get a fine powder.
3. Heat the oil in a big non-stick wok or saucepan using high heat, put in the mustard seeds and asafoetida, and stir approximately one minute. Put in the mangoes, ground chile-fenugreek mixture, and salt, and cook using high heat, approximately one minute.
4. Reduce the heat to moderate to low, cover the pan and cook, stirring intermittently, until the mangoes are soft, approximately fifteen minutes. Allow to cool and move to a big sanitized jar. This pickle can be stored safely at room temperature for approximately seven days or approximately three months in a fridge. Serve chilled or at room temperature.

GRATED MANGO PICKLE Ⓥ

This recipe is called "Kaddukas aam ka achaar" in Hindi

Yield: Approximately 2 cups

Ingredients:

- ¼ teaspoon ground asafoetida
- ⅓ cup peanut oil
- 1 tablespoon black mustard seeds
- 1 teaspoon cayenne pepper, or to taste
- 1 teaspoon ground fenugreek seeds
- 3 large unripe green mangoes (about ¾ pound each), washed and wiped dry
- 5 to 7 dried red chile peppers, such as chile de arbol, broken

Directions:

1. Using a vegetable peeler, peel the mangoes, then grate the fruit around the center seed of each mango. Throw away the center seeds. Put the fenugreek and asafoetida in a small-sized cast-iron skillet and roast using moderate heat, stirring and swaying the pan, until seems slightly darker, approximately one minute.
2. Heat the oil in a big non-stick wok or saucepan using moderate to high heat, put in the red chile peppers and cook, stirring, until seems slightly darker, approximately one minute. Put in the mustard seeds; they should splutter when they touch the hot oil, so reduce the heat and cover the pan until the spluttering diminishes.
3. Put in the grated mango and cayenne pepper and cook, stirring, until a golden colour is achieved, approximately five to seven minutes. Stir in the roasted fenugreek and asafoetida, stir approximately one minute and remove from the heat. Allow to cool and move to a big sanitized jar. This pickle stays fresh approximately seven days at room temperature or approximately six months in a fridge. Serve chilled or at room temperature.

LIME AND LEMON PICKLES

BASIC LEMON PICKLE Ⓥ

This recipe is called "Nimboo ka achaar" in Hindi

Yield: Approximately 4 cups

Ingredients:

- ¼ cup salt
- ½ cup peeled and minced fresh ginger
- 1 small piece muslin or 4 layers cheesecloth (sufficient to cover the mouth of the jar)
- 2 tablespoons crudely crushed ajwain seeds
- 20 to 24 fresh limes (about 2 pounds)
- 4 cups fresh lime or lemon juice (from 20 additional limes)

Directions:

1. Rinse and wipe dry the limes. Cut each one into 8 wedges and place in a big sterile glass jar. Stir in the ginger, salt, and ajwain seeds, cover the jar using the palm of your hand or the lid, and shake rapidly to combine.
2. Uncover, put in the lime juice, and shake the jar once more. (The juice should cover the limes by about ½ inch; if not, add some more lime juice.) Cover the jar with the muslin, locking it using a rubber band, and if there is a warm sunny spot in the kitchen, put it there, else put it outdoors where there it can get some sun. (bring the jar indoors in the evening if you're keeping it outdoors.)
3. Sway the jar a couple of times per day, until the lime wedges are soft and light buff in color, and the juices are thick, fifteen to twenty days. This pickle can be stored safely at room temperature for more than a decade!.

SWEET AND SOUR FRESH LIME PICKLE Ⓥ

This recipe is called "Khatta-meetha nimboo ka achaar" in Hindi

Yield: Approximately 4 cups

Ingredients:

- ¼ cup salt
- 1 cup sugar
- 1 small piece muslin or 4 layers cheesecloth (sufficient to cover the mouth of the jar)
- 1½ to 2 tablespoons cayenne pepper, or to taste
- 2 tablespoons ajwain seeds, crudely ground
- 20 fresh limes (about 2 pounds)
- 4 cups fresh lime or lemon juice (from 20 additional limes)

Directions:

1. Rinse and wipe dry the limes. Cut each one into 8 wedges, and place in a big sterile glass jar. Stir in the sugar, salt, cayenne pepper, and ajwain seeds, cover the jar using the palm of your hand or the lid, and shake rapidly to combine.
2. Uncover, put in the lime juice, and shake the jar once more. (The juice should cover the limes by about ½ inch; if not, add some more lime juice.) Cover the jar with the muslin, locking it using a rubber band, and if there is a warm sunny spot in the kitchen, put it there, else put it outdoors where there it can get some sun. (bring the jar indoors in the evening if you're keeping it outdoors.)
3. Sway the jar a couple of times per day, until the lime or lemon wedges are soft and light buff in color, and the juices are thick, fifteen to twenty days. This pickle can be stored safely at room temperature for more than a decade!.

CRUSHED LEMON AND FRESH RED CHILE PEPPER PICKLE Ⓥ

This recipe is called "Pissa nimboo-laal mirch ka achaar" in Hindi

Yield: Approximately 2 cups

Ingredients:

- ¼ cup salt
- 1 small piece muslin or 4 layers cheesecloth (sufficient to cover the mouth of the jar)

- 1 tablespoon ajwain seeds, crudely ground
- 12 to fifteen fresh red or green chile peppers, stemmed
- 12 to fifteen thin-skinned, seedless lemons or limes (about 1 pound)

Directions:

1. Rinse and wipe dry the lemons or limes, then crudely cut them, with the rind, and remove any seeds. Move to a food processor, along with the chile peppers, and process until minced.
2. Put in the ajwain seeds and salt, and process once more until the desired smoothness is achieved. Move to a sterile glass jar. Cover the jar with the muslin, locking it using a rubber band, and if there is a warm sunny spot in the kitchen, put it there, else put it outdoors where there it can get some sun. (bring the jar indoors in the evening if you're keeping it outdoors.)
3. Sway the jar a couple of times per day, until the pickle is light buff in color and the juices are thick, approximately seven days. This pickle can be stored safely at room temperature for approximately a year.

GINGER-LEMON PICKLE Ⓥ

This recipe is called "Adrak nimboo" in Hindi

Yield: Approximately 2 cups

Ingredients:

- ½ pound fresh ginger, peeled and cut into 2-inch matchsticks
- 1 tablespoon salt
- 1½ cups fresh lemon or lime juice (from 7 to 10 limes)
- 2 teaspoons ajwain seeds, crudely crushed

Directions:

1. Put the ginger in a big non-reactive container. Put in the salt and mix thoroughly. Let sit for about two hours at room temperature. (By then the salt will have drawn out the juices from the ginger, and the container will have a fair amount of juice.)

2. Put in the ajwain seeds and lemon juice and set aside at room temperature until the ginger sticks are pink, 2 to four hours. Move to a sanitized glass jar and store in the refrigerator, approximately six months. Serve chilled or at room temperature.

MINCED GINGER-LIME PICKLE Ⓥ

This recipe is called "Pissa hua adrak nimboo ka achaar" in Hindi

Yield: Approximately 2 cups

Ingredients:

- ¼ cup salt, or to taste
- 1 cup fresh lime juice (from 5 to 7 limes)
- 1 pound fresh ginger, peeled and cut crosswise into thin round slices
- 1½ tablespoons ajwain seeds, crudely ground
- 15 to 20 fresh green chile peppers, such as serrano, crudely chopped

Directions:

1. Using a food processor or a blender, combine and pulse the ginger and green chile peppers until minced.
2. Move to a big sanitized jar and add all the rest of the ingredients. Cover the jar using the palm of your hand or the lid and shake rapidly to combine.
3. Allow to sit at room temperature about four hours. This pickle stays fresh about six months in a fridge. Served chilled or at room temperature.

GREEN CHILE PEPPER PICKLES

VINEGAR-MARINATED GREEN CHILE PEPPERS Ⓥ

This recipe is called "Sirkae vaali hari mirch" in Hindi

Yield: Approximately 1½ cups

Ingredients:

- ½ cup distilled white vinegar
- 1 tablespoon dried mint leaves
- 1 tablespoon salt, or to taste
- 1 tablespoon sugar
- 1 tablespoon Tamarind Paste
- 15 to 20 fresh green chile peppers, such as serrano, thinly chopped

Directions:

1. Ready the tamarind paste. Next, place the chile peppers in a small non-reactive container. Put in the salt and mix thoroughly. Let sit for about two hours at room temperature. (By then the salt will have drawn out the juices from the chile peppers, and the container will have a fair amount of juice.)
2. Stir in the vinegar, tamarind paste, sugar, and mint. Refrigerate at least 24 hours before using. Next, move to a sanitized glass jar and store in the fridge for approximately a year. Serve chilled or at room temperature.

PICKLED CHILE PEPPER WITH TAMARIND Ⓥ

This recipe is called "Hari mirch aur imli ka achaar" in Hindi

Yield: Approximately 1½ cups

Ingredients:

- ¼ cup white urad beans (dhulli urad dal), dry-roasted and crudely ground (See the dry-roasting section in Introduction)
- ⅓ cup Tamarind Paste
- ½ pound fresh green chile peppers, such as serranos, crudely chopped
- 1 large clove fresh garlic, chopped
- 1 tablespoon cumin seeds
- 1 tablespoon sesame seeds, dry-roasted and crudely ground (See the dry-roasting section in Introduction)
- 1 tablespoon sugar
- 1¼ cups water
- 1½ teaspoons salt, or to taste
- 2 tablespoons coriander seeds

Directions:

1. Ready the dal, sesame seeds, and tamarind paste. Next, place the green chile peppers, dal, garlic, tamarind paste, and water in a non-stick saucepan and bring to a boil using high heat. Reduce the heat to moderate to low, cover the pan and cook approximately five minutes. Put in the coriander, cumin, sugar, and salt, and continue to cook until the peppers are soft, approximately eight to ten minutes.
2. Move to a food processor or a blender and process until a smooth paste is achieved. Transfer to a serving container, lightly stir in the sesame seeds with some of them visible as a decoration, and serve. Or move to a sanitized glass jar and store in the fridge for approximately six months. Serve chilled or at room temperature.

FIERY GREEN CHILE PEPPER PICKLE Ⓥ

This recipe is called "Prabha ka hari mirch ka achaar" in Hindi

Yield: Approximately 1½ cups

If you like it hot, this might be the pickle for you!

Ingredients:

- ½ cup mustard or peanut oil

- ½ teaspoon ground turmeric
- 1 pound fresh green chile peppers, such as serrano, cut into ¼-inch diagonal slices
- 1 tablespoon citric acid or 2 tablespoons distilled white vinegar
- 1 tablespoon fennel seeds
- 1 to 2 tablespoons salt
- 2 teaspoons fenugreek seeds

Directions:

1. In a mortar and pestle (or a spice or coffee grinder), crudely mix together and grind the fenugreek and fennel seeds. Move to a container and stir in the turmeric.
2. Heat the oil in a big non-stick wok or saucepan using moderate to high heat. Reduce the heat to low, put in the ground spices and salt, and stir a few seconds. Put in the green chile peppers and cook until they are crisp-tender, three to five minutes. Stir in the citric acid (or vinegar) and cook another two to three minutes. Allow to cool, then move to a sanitized glass jar and store in the fridge for approximately a year. Serve chilled or at room temperature.

OTHER VEGETABLE PICKLES

CRUNCHY CUCUMBER PICKLE Ⓥ

This recipe is called "Kheerae ka achaar" in Hindi

Yield: Approximately 2 cups

The Indian version of a popular American pickle!

Ingredients:

- ⅛ teaspoon ground asafoetida
- ¼ cup distilled white vinegar
- 1 medium onion, cut into ½-inch pieces

- 1 tablespoon dried curry leaves
- 1 teaspoon black mustard seeds
- 1 teaspoon salt, or to taste
- 2 large cloves fresh garlic, minced
- 2 tablespoons peanut oil
- 3 to 5 dried red chile peppers, such as chiles de arbol, with stems
- 3 to 5 fresh green chile peppers, such as serrano, halved lengthwise
- 4 to 5 small seedless cucumbers (about ¾ pound), diagonally chopped

Directions:

1. In a container, toss the cucumbers with salt and allow to sweat approximately one hour.
2. Heat the oil in a big non-stick wok or saucepan over moderate heat and cook the red chile peppers about half a minute. Put in the green chile peppers and stir for about half a minute. Put in the mustard seeds; they should splutter when they touch the hot oil, so reduce the heat and cover the pan until the spluttering diminishes.
3. Mix in the asafoetida and curry leaves, then Put in the onion and garlic, and cook, stirring, until barely softened, approximately three minutes. Put in the cucumber with all the juices and cook, stirring, approximately one minute.
4. Put in the vinegar and boil using high heat approximately one minute. Turn off the heat. Allow to cool, move to a sterile glass jar, and refrigerate at least two days before you serve. This pickle stays fresh about six months in a fridge. Serve chilled or at room temperature.

CAULIFLOWER-CARROT WATER PICKLE

Ⓥ

This recipe is called "Gobhi-gajjar ka paani wala achaar" in Hindi

Yield: Approximately 2 cups

Ingredients:

- ⅛ teaspoon ground turmeric
- ¼ teaspoon cayenne pepper, or to taste

- 1 (1-inch) piece fresh ginger, peeled, cut in half lengthwise, and thinly chopped
- 1 pound cauliflower, cut into 1½-inch florets, stems discarded
- 1 small piece muslin or 4 layers cheesecloth (sufficient to cover the mouth of the jar)
- 1½ teaspoons salt, or to taste
- 2 cups water
- 2 teaspoons black mustard seeds, ground
- 3 tablespoons distilled white vinegar
- 3 to 4 small carrots, peeled and diagonally chopped
- 8 to 10 fresh green chile peppers, such as serrano, stemmed and halved lengthwise

Directions:

1. Put the vegetables and water in a moderate-sized saucepan and bring to boil using high heat. Boil half a minute, then cover the pan and remove from the heat. Set aside approximately one minute. Move to a big sanitized glass jar with a wide mouth and stir in all the rest of the ingredients.

2. Cover the jar with the muslin, locking it using a rubber band, and if there is a warm sunny spot in the kitchen, put it there, else put it outdoors where there it can get some sun. (bring the jar indoors in the evening if you're keeping it outdoors.) Sway the jar a couple of times per day, until the vegetables are sour, two to four days. This pickle can be stored safely at room temperature for approximately seven days and about six months in the refrigerator, getting more and more pungent as time passes. Serve chilled or at room temperature.

SPICY CRANBERRY PICKLE Ⓥ

This recipe is called "Karonda achaar" in Hindi

Yield: Approximately 2 cups

Ingredients:

- ¼ cup Bengali Five Spices (Panch-Phoran) (make your own using the recipe in the spice blend section, or buy from a store)
- ½ cup mustard oil

- ½ teaspoon ground turmeric
- 1 (12-ounce) package fresh cranberries, washed
- 1 tablespoon citric acid or 2 tablespoons distilled white vinegar
- 1 tablespoon salt, or to taste

Directions:

1. In a mortar and pestle, crudely grind the 5-spices mixture. Stir in the turmeric and salt.
2. Heat the oil in a big non-stick wok or saucepan using moderate to high heat until smoking. Reduce the heat to low, put in the spices, and stir a few seconds. Put in the cranberries and cook until they are crisp-tender, approximately ten to twelve minutes. Stir in the citric acid (or vinegar) and cook another two to three minutes. Allow to cool, move to a sterile jar and store in the refrigerator, approximately a year.
3. Serve chilled or at room temperature.

ONION PICKLE Ⓥ

This recipe is called "Pyaz ka achaar" in Hindi

Yield: Approximately 2 cups

Ingredients:

- ½ cup mustard or olive oil
- 1 pound pearl onions, peeled
- 1 small piece muslin or 4 layers cheesecloth (sufficient to cover the mouth of the jar)
- 1 tablespoon fennel seeds
- 1 tablespoon fenugreek seeds
- 1 tablespoon salt, or to taste
- 1 teaspoon cayenne pepper, or to taste
- 1 teaspoon ground turmeric
- 1½ teaspoons kalonji seeds
- 2 teaspoons black peppercorns

Directions:

1. Make a cross-cut at the base of each onion, going 75% of the way to the top. Gently open the cuts and stuff a pinch of salt in each one. Save any leftover salt for future use. Using a spice or coffee grinder, very crudely mix together and grind the fenugreek, fennel, peppercorns and kalonji. Move to a container and stir in the turmeric, cayenne pepper, and the reserved salt.
2. Heat the oil in a big non-stick wok or saucepan using moderate to high heat and put in the spice mixture; it should sizzle when they touch the hot oil. Put in the onions and cook approximately five minutes, ensuring all the onions are thoroughly coated with the spice mixture.
3. Allow to cool and move to a sterile glass jar. Cover the jar with the muslin, locking it using a rubber band, and if there is a warm sunny spot in the kitchen, put it there, else put it outdoors where there it can get some sun. (bring the jar indoors in the evening if you're keeping it outdoors.) Sway the jar a couple of times per day, until the spices are plump and soft and the onions are crisp-tender, three to five days. The onions will release some juices; that is quite normal. Store about ten days at room temperature and about six months in a fridge. The onions keep getting stronger over time.

TURNIP PICKLE Ⓥ

This recipe is called "Shalgam ka achaar" in Hindi

Yield: Approximately 4 cups

Ingredients:

- 1 small piece muslin or 4 layers cheesecloth (sufficient to cover the mouth of the jar)
- 1 tablespoon black mustard seeds, crudely ground
- 1 tablespoon salt
- 1 teaspoon cayenne pepper, or to taste
- 1½ pounds turnips, cut into 1-inch pieces (peeled or unpeeled)
- 2 to 3 cups water

Directions:

1. Bring the water to a boil in a big pot. Put in the turnips and boil approximately one minute. Drain and move the turnips to a tray coated using paper towels and air-dry them about ten minutes.

2. Move to a big sanitized glass jar with a wide mouth and put in the mustard seeds, salt, and cayenne pepper. Toss well, then cover the jar with the muslin locking it using a rubber band, and set aside at room temperature until the turnips turn sour, five to seven days. To cure faster, place in the sun during the day, bringing the pickle inside in the evening. Shake the jar once or twice a day. This pickle can be stored safely at room temperature for approximately seven days (longer in the refrigerator), getting more and more pungent as time passes.

TURNIP & CAULIFLOWER PICKLE Ⓥ

This recipe is called "Shalgam gobhi ka achaar" in Hindi

Yield: Approximately 8 to 10 cups

Ingredients:

- ¼ cup black mustard seeds, crudely ground
- ½ cup mustard oil
- ½ cup sugar
- 1 cup distilled white vinegar
- 1 small piece muslin or 4 layers cheesecloth (sufficient to cover the mouth of the jar)
- 1 teaspoon cayenne pepper, or to taste
- 1¼ pounds small turnips, peeled and cut into ¼-inch thick slices
- 1½ pounds cauliflower, cut into 1½-inch florets, stems discarded
- 2 ounces fresh garlic cloves, peeled
- 2 tablespoons garam masala
- 2 teaspoons ground paprika
- 3 ounces fresh ginger, peeled and cut into thin round slices
- 3 tablespoons salt
- 3 to 4 cups water

Directions:

1. Bring the water to a boil in a big pot. Put in the turnips and cauliflower and blanch approximately one minute; do not allow them to soften. Drain and move to a tray coated using paper towels and air-dry them about ten minutes. Process the ginger and garlic Using a food processor or a blender until a fine paste is achieved.

2. Heat the oil in a big non-stick wok or saucepan using moderate to high heat and put in the ginger-garlic paste. Cook, stirring, over moderate heat until rich golden in color, approximately four minutes. Put in the garam masala and stir for approximately half a minute.

3. Put in the vegetables and salt and cook, stirring, approximately two to three minutes. Put in the sugar and cook, stirring, approximately one minute. Remove from heat and stir in the mustard seeds, cayenne pepper, paprika, and vinegar. Move to a large, sanitized glass jar with a wide mouth. Cover the jar with the muslin, locking it using a rubber band, and if there is a warm sunny spot in the kitchen, put it there, else put it outdoors where there it can get some sun. (bring the jar indoors in the evening if you're keeping it outdoors.) Sway the jar a couple of times per day, until the turnips are sour, five to seven days. (Taste, and if not sour enough, cover and set aside longer.) This pickle can be stored safely at room temperature for approximately three months, getting more and more pungent over time.

MIXED VEGETABLE PICKLE Ⓥ

This recipe is called "Sabzi ka achaar" in Hindi

Yield: Approximately 4 cups

Ingredients:

- ½ cup distilled white vinegar
- ½ cup vegetable oil
- ½ teaspoon cayenne pepper, or to taste
- ½ teaspoon ground paprika
- ½ teaspoon ground turmeric
- 1 (15-ounce) can tomato sauce
- 1 pound carrots, finely chopped
- 1 pound cauliflower, finely chopped
- 1 tablespoon cumin seeds

- 1 tablespoon fenugreek seeds
- 1 tablespoon salt, or to taste
- 2 large heads fresh garlic, peeled and chopped
- 2 tablespoons fennel seeds
- 2 teaspoons kalonji seeds
- 5 to 7 fresh green chile peppers, such as serrano, diagonally chopped

Directions:

1. Heat the oil in a big non-stick wok or saucepan using moderate to high heat and put in the fennel, fenugreek, cumin, and kalonji seeds. They should sizzle when they touch the hot oil. Swiftly put in the turmeric, stir for approximately half a minute, and put in the vegetables, garlic, and green chile peppers. Cook, stirring, until the vegetables are lightly golden, approximately five minutes.
2. Put in the vinegar, tomato sauce, salt, paprika, and cayenne pepper, and bring to a boil using high heat. Reduce the heat to moderate to low, cover the pan, and simmer until the vegetables are crisp-tender, approximately seven minutes. Allow to cool, move to a big sanitized jar, and store in the fridge for approximately ten days. Serve chilled or at room temperature.

EGGPLANT AND MALANGA ROOT PICKLE Ⓥ

This recipe is called "Baingan-kachaalu ka achaar" in Hindi

Yield: Approximately 4 cups

Ingredients:

- 1 pound malanga root or taro root
- 1 pound small Indian eggplants or Chinese eggplants, cut into 2-inch pieces
- 1 tablespoon fennel seeds, crudely ground
- 1 tablespoon salt
- 1 teaspoon cayenne pepper, or to taste
- 1½ to 2 cups mustard oil
- 2 tablespoons black mustard seeds, crudely ground
- 2 teaspoons ground turmeric

Directions:

1. Make a cross-cut at the base of each eggplant, going 75% of the way to the top. Put in a saucepan along with 2 cups water and 1 teaspoon turmeric, and bring to a boil using high heat. Reduce the heat to moderate to low, cover the pan, and simmer until the eggplants are half cooked (crisp-tender), approximately seven minutes. Drain the eggplants over a container and reserve about ¾ cup water.
2. In the same saucepan, place the malanga root and about 4 cups of fresh water, and bring to a boil using high heat. Reduce the heat to moderate to low, cover the pan, and simmer until the malanga root is soft, pouring in additional water if it evaporates, approximately fifteen minutes. Remove from the water, allow to cool down, then peel and cut into 3/⁴-inch pieces. Throw away the water.
3. In a large container, combine the eggplants, malanga root, mustard and fennel seeds, salt, cayenne pepper, the rest of the 1 teaspoon turmeric, and mix thoroughly, ensuring all the vegetables are thoroughly coated.
4. Heat the oil in a small saucepan using moderate to high heat until smoking. Turn off the heat, add to the container with the vegetables, and mix once more. Allow to cool and move to a big sanitized jar. Make sure there is minimum ½ inch of oil on the surface, if not, then heat and add some more. Cover the jar with the muslin, locking it using a rubber band, and place in a warm, sunny spot in the kitchen, or outside in the sun, swaying the jar a couple of times per day for two days.
5. 5. Stir in the reserved eggplant water and shake the jar once more. Put in a warm, sunny spot in the kitchen, or outside in the sun again, swaying the jar a couple of times per day until the vegetables are very soft and tangy, about one week. This pickle can be stored safely at room temperature for approximately one month, and in the fridge for approximately six months. Serve chilled or at room temperature.

STARTERS AND SNACKS

We Indians love snacks. If you take a stroll in a market in India, you will find food stalls all over the place. During peak hours, will probably get to see people waiting in lines to get their hands on the snacks being sold at these food stalls. Needless to say, India has a culture of snacks.

In this section we will take a look at a few of the most popular snacks Indians enjoy. Almost every snack recipe in this section is best enjoyed with a chutney on the side. I've already listed more than 40 chutney recipes in the previous section, so make sure you go through those too.

You may or may not find a chutney recommendation in the recipes that follow, so feel free to play around and experiment.

Ⓥ= Vegan Ⓟ= Quick Pressure Cooker Recipe

SPICY RELISH MIXES

FRIED TARO CHIPS Ⓥ

This recipe is called "Tali arbi kae lacchae" in Hindi

Yield: 4 to 6 servings

Ingredients:

- ⅛ teaspoon ground asafoetida
- ½ teaspoon cayenne pepper, or to taste
- ½ teaspoon salt, or to taste
- 1 pound taro root, peeled and cut into thin julienne sticks
- 1½ to 2 cups coconut or peanut oil for deep-frying

Directions:

1. Heat the oil in a big wok using moderate to high heat until it achieves 325°F to 350°F on a frying thermometer or when a small piece of taro root dropped into the hot oil surges to the surface of the oil after fifteen to 20 seconds.

2. Put in the taro root sticks in 2 or 3 batches, adding as many as the wok can hold simultaneously. Fry, stirring and turning, until crunchy and golden, approximately one minute per batch. Move to paper towels with a slotted spatula to drain.

3. Allow to cool and remove all but 1 teaspoon of oil from the wok. Heat the oil and put in the asafoetida, cayenne pepper, and salt. Put in the taro root sticks and mix thoroughly. Serve hot.

GRAM FLOUR FRIED PEANUTS Ⓥ

This recipe is called "Besan-tali moong-phalli" in Hindi

Yield: Approximately 2 cups

Feel free to use any nut of your choice instead of peanuts!

Ingredients:

- ⅛ teaspoon baking soda
- ⅛ teaspoon ground asafoetida
- ½ 1 teaspoon salt, or to taste
- ½ cup chickpea flour
- ½ to 1 teaspoon cayenne pepper, or to taste
- 1 teaspoon ground ginger
- 1½ to 2 cups peanut oil for deep-frying
- 2 cups shelled raw peanuts, with or without red skin
- 3 tablespoons fresh lemon juice

Directions:

1. Put the chickpea flour into a sifter or a fine-mesh strainer and sift the flour into a moderate-sized container. Stir in the ginger, salt, cayenne pepper, baking soda, and asafoetida. Stir in the peanuts and then Put in the lemon juice and mix with clean fingers, ensuring the peanuts are coated with a thick batter (add 1 tablespoon water, if required).

2. Heat the oil in a big wok or skillet using moderate to high heat until it achieves 325°F to 350°F on a frying thermometer or until a small bit of batter dropped into the hot oil bubbles and surges to the surface of the oil instantly. Next, Put

in the batter-coated peanuts, piece by piece (or by the handful), adding as many as the wok can hold simultaneously. Separate them swiftly with a fork or a slotted spatula and fry, stirring and turning, until crunchy and golden, approximately one minute. Replicate the process for the rest of the peanuts. Move to paper towels with a slotted spatula to drain. Allow to cool and serve, or store in an airtight vessel in the fridge up to half a month.

SALTED CASHEWS Ⓥ

This recipe is called "Namkeen kaaju" in Hindi

Yield: Approximately 2 cups

Ingredients:

- ¼ teaspoon freshly ground black pepper, or to taste
- ¼ teaspoon salt, or to taste
- ½ cup peanut oil for deep-frying
- 2 cups raw cashews

Directions:

1. Heat the oil in a moderate-sized non-stick wok or saucepan over moderate heat and fry, stirring and turning the cashews until a golden colour is achieved, approximately one minute. Before you take them out of the wok, drain thoroughly. (The nuts will stick to paper, so don't use paper towels to drain.)
2. Move to a container and swiftly stir in the salt and pepper and toss well, ensuring the cashews are coated thoroughly.
3. Allow to cool and harden for a while before you serve, or cool to room temperature, move to an airtight vessel and store fifteen to twenty days at room temperature or approximately three months in a fridge.

SALTY CEREAL MIX Ⓥ

This recipe is called "Mila-jula namkeen" in Hindi

Yield: Approximately 8 cups

Ingredients:

- ¼ teaspoon ground asafoetida
- ¼ teaspoon ground ginger
- ½ cup crudely chopped raw cashews
- ½ cup finely chopped fresh cilantro, including soft stems
- ½ cup mixed melon seeds or shelled raw sunflower seeds
- ½ cup shelled raw peanuts, with red skins on
- ½ teaspoon cayenne pepper, or to taste
- 1 teaspoon black mustard seeds
- 1½ tablespoons Chaat Masala (Homemade or store-bought), or to taste
- 1½ teaspoons citric acid
- 2 cups canned potato sticks
- 2 cups corn flake cereal
- 2 tablespoons dried curry leaves
- 3 cups puffed rice cereal
- 3 tablespoons peanut oil

Directions:

1. Ready the chaat masala. Heat 1 tablespoon oil in a big wok or skillet and cook the peanuts and cashews over moderate heat, stirring as required, until it starts to look golden and releases its fragrance, two to five minutes. Move to a container.
2. Another way is to roast in the oven at 350°F until a mild golden colour and fragrance is achieved, ten to fifteen minutes.
3. Take the same pan again and put in the melon (or sunflower) seeds to the wok and dry-roast until a golden colour is achieved, approximately one minute. Move to the peanut container.
4. Heat the rest of the 2 tablespoons oil using moderate to high heat and put in the mustard seeds and asafoetida. They should splutter when they touch the hot oil, so cover the pan and reduce the heat until the spluttering diminishes. Stir in the cayenne pepper and ginger, and then add first the cilantro, then the curry leaves, chaat masala, and citric acid, and stir for approximately half a minute.
5. Put in the puffed rice cereal, corn flakes, potato sticks, roasted nuts, and seeds. Reduce the heat to low and cook, stirring intermittently, approximately five

minutes, ensuring everything is coated thoroughly with the spices. Allow to cool completely. Move it to an airtight vessel and store at room temperature approximately sixty days.

SPICY MIXED NUTS AND SEEDS Ⓥ

This recipe is called "Masaledaar maevae" in Hindi

Yield: Approximately 2½ cups

Feel free to use your favourite nuts and seeds in this recipe instead of the ones I use.

Ingredients:

- ¼ teaspoon black salt (not compulsory)
- ¼ teaspoon cayenne pepper, or to taste
- ½ cup mixed shelled raw seeds, such as sunflower, pumpkin, melon
- ½ cup peanut oil for deep-frying
- 1 teaspoon cumin seeds, dry-roasted and crudely ground (See the dry-roasting section in Introduction)
- 1½ to 2 teaspoons Chaat Masala (Homemade or store-bought)
- 2 cups mixed shelled raw nuts, such as almonds, cashews, peanuts, pistachios

Directions:

1. Ready the cumin seeds and chaat masala. Next, in a small-sized container, combine the cumin seeds, chaat masala, cayenne pepper, and black salt.
2. Heat the oil in a medium-size non-stick wok or saucepan over moderate heat and fry the nuts until a golden colour is achieved, approximately one minute. Before you take them out of the wok, drain thoroughly. (Do not drain them on paper towels, or the spices will not adhere.) Move them to a medium container, swiftly Put in the spice mixture and toss well, ensuring that the nuts are thoroughly coated.
3. Remove all the oil from the wok, then in whatever oil remains on the wok surface, stir-fry the seeds using moderate to low heat until the seeds are fragrant and golden, approximately one minute. Put into the spiced nuts and toss together. Taste and adjust seasonings. (Keep in mind that the warm nuts will be soft, but will harden as they cool.) Allow to cool completely then serve

or move to an airtight vessel and store fifteen to twenty days at room temperature or approximately three months in a fridge.

SPICY PRESSED RICE FLAKE MIX Ⓥ

This recipe is called "Chivda" in Hindi

Yield: Approximately 5 cups

Pressed rice flakes are easily available in Indian markets and online. It is called "poha" in Hindi.

Ingredients:

- ⅛ teaspoon ground alum
- ¼ teaspoon ground turmeric
- ½ cup dried split yellow chickpeas (channa dal), sorted and washed in 3 to 4 changes of water
- ½ teaspoon ground fenugreek seeds
- 1 (3-by-1-inch) piece dried coconut (kopra), thinly chopped (not compulsory)
- 1 cup shelled raw peanuts, with or without the red skin
- 1 teaspoon cayenne pepper, or to taste
- 1 teaspoon citric acid
- 1 teaspoon ground coriander
- 1 teaspoon ground cumin
- 1 teaspoon salt, or to taste
- 1 teaspoon sugar
- 1 to 3 fresh green chile peppers, such as serrano, minced with seeds
- 1½ tablespoons finely chopped fresh curry leaves
- 2 cups pressed rice flakes (poha)
- 2 tablespoons finely chopped fresh cilantro, including soft stems
- 2 to 3 cups peanut oil for deep-frying

Directions:

1. Put the dal in water to cover by 1 inch. Stir in the alum and soak overnight. Next, drain and spread the dal on a tray lined with several layers of paper towels or cheesecloth until completely dry, one to two hours. Stir a few times

using your fingers to make sure they are thoroughly dried. (Otherwise, rest of the water will cause spluttering when the dal is deep-fried.)

2. Heat the oil in a big wok or saucepan over moderate heat until a few rice flakes dropped into the hot oil bubble and rise to the top instantly. Put the rice flakes in a big fine-mesh metal strainer (in 2 batches, if required) and place the strainer with the rice flakes in it into the hot oil. Fry, stirring the rice flakes in the strainer until they are crisp and very lightly golden, approximately one minute. Move to a container coated using paper towels. Put in the turmeric and ½ teaspoon salt to the rice flakes, and toss lightly.

3. Same way, fry the coconut slices (if using), then the dal, and finally, the peanuts. Mix each into the rice flakes. Put in the rest of the ½ teaspoon salt and toss once more.

4. Take the oil out of the wok while leaving approximately one tablespoon in it . Heat the oil on moderate to low heat and cook the green chile peppers, cilantro, and curry leaves, stirring, until a golden colour is achieved and crisp, approximately five minutes.

5. Put in the citric acid, cumin, coriander, cayenne pepper, fenugreek seeds, and sugar to the wok, and stir approximately one minute. Next, Put in the fried ingredients and mix lightly until they are coated thoroughly with the spices. Keep uncovered at all times, and cool to room temperature. Store in an airtight vessel up to sixty days.

SPICY THIN CRISPY FLATBREADS Ⓥ

This recipe is called "Paapad" in Hindi

Yield: 1 to 2 paapad

Ready-made paapads are easily available in Indian markets, and even online. All you need to to these pre-made paapads is fry or roast them, depending on your preference. These are extremely cheap, and in India, are a common side snacks enjoyed with rice and curry dishes. These can also be eaten just by themselves. In India, people mostly buy raw paapads and cook them immediately before eating. Try out the different brands of paapads available to you and pick your favourite one.

Ingredients:

- Raw Paapads (buy online or from Indian stores)

Directions:

1. Flame Roast using tongs: hold each paapad over the flame and roast it, starting with the edges and moving toward the center.
2. Or, put inside preheated pven until crisp—maximum 35 seconds—ensuring the edges do not burn.
3. Or, deep fry and drain thoroughly before serving.
4. Or, microwave on high power for a minute (easiest and most convenient method).

MATHIYA

Mathiya or Mathri is a West Indian snack from Rajasthan. It is a kind of flaky biscuit that is commonly enjoyed with tea.

AJWAIN SEED MATHIYA Ⓥ

This recipe is called "Ajwaini mathri" in Hindi

Yield: 16 pieces

Ingredients:

- ¼ cup canola oil
- ¼ cup semolina
- ½ cup warm water
- ½ to 1 teaspoon crudely ground black pepper + 16 black peppercorns
- 1 teaspoon crudely ground ajwain seeds
- 1 teaspoon salt, or to taste
- 1½ to 2 cups vegetable oil for deep-frying
- 2 cups all-purpose flour
- 2 tablespoons melted ghee

Directions:

1. Put the flour, semolina, oil, ghee, ajwain seeds, ground pepper, and salt in a mixing container and rub lightly with clean fingers to mix. Next, Put in the water, slowly and gradually, and mix until the dough gathers into a semi-firm ball that does not stick to your fingers. (Lightly coat your fingers with oil, if required.)

2. Split the dough into 16 identical portions and, use a rolling pin to roll out each one into a thin 3- to 4-inch disc that is approximately ⅛-inch thick. If the dough sticks to the rolling surface, coat mildly with oil; do not dust with dry flour.

3. Use the tip of a knife to poke a few holes or make ¼-inch slits all over in each round. This will ensure that the dough doesnt get puffed while frying. Put one peppercorn in the center of each mathri and push it in tightly.

4. Heat the oil in a big wok or skillet over moderate heat until it reaches 300°F to 325°F on a frying thermometer, or when a small drop of dough begins to bubble while it is still immersed. (Reduce the heat if it rises instantly or browns.) Put in the discs, as many as the wok can comfortably hold simultaneously, and fry, turning as required, until crunchy and appears mildly golden. Do not brown them and ensure the centers are crisp. Drain using paper towels. Allow to cool completely, and store in airtight containers at room temperature approximately sixty days.

MUNG BEAN PUFFED PASTRIES Ⓥ

This recipe is called "Mung dal kachauri" in Hindi

Yield: Approximately 30 pieces

The "kachauri" is a highly popular spicy Indian Pastry.

Ingredients:

- ¼ cup lukewarm water, or as required
- ¼ teaspoon ground asafoetida
- ½ cup vegetable oil
- ½ teaspoon black peppercorns
- ½ teaspoon ground turmeric
- ¾ cup dried yellow mung beans (dhulli mung dal), sorted and washed in 3 to 4 changes of water
- 1 tablespoon coriander

- 1 teaspoon cumin seeds
- 1 teaspoon hot red pepper flakes, or to taste
- 1½ tablespoons fennel seeds
- 2 black cardamom pods, seeds only
- 2 tablespoons chickpea flour
- 2 teaspoons salt, or to taste
- 2 to 3 cups peanut oil for deep-frying
- 3 cups all-purpose flour
- 5 whole cloves

Directions:

1. Immerse the dal in water to cover by 2 inches, and drain. Next, make the filling: Using a food processor or a blender, process the dal to make a coarse paste. In a spice or a coffee grinder, crudely mix together and grind all the whole spices (fennel to cardamom).
2. Heat ¼ cup of the vegetable oil in a big non-stick wok or saucepan using moderate to high heat and put in the asafoetida, then the ground spices, and stir for approximately half a minute. Stir in the chickpea flour and stir another half a minute.
3. Put in the dal paste and cook over moderate heat, stirring and breaking any lumps, approximately ten minutes. Put in the salt and stir to mix thoroughly. Allow to cool and divide equally into 30 portions (about 1 tablespoon each). Make a ball of each portion and save for later. If the balls seem to fall apart, this means the filling is too dry; moisten it with 1 to 2 tablespoons hot water.
4. Make the dough: In a moderate-sized container, using clean fingers, rub together the flour, turmeric, and the rest of the ¼ cup oil until well mixed. Add sufficient water to make a soft and pliable dough, adding slowly and gradually. Put the dough on a cutting board and pound lightly with a meat mallet approximately two minutes. Turn the dough over during the two minutes to pound different sections. This makes the dough very elastic. Split the dough equally into 30 portions.
5. Assemble the kachauries: In a small-sized container, make a paste of 2 tablespoons all-purpose flour and 1 tablespoon water and keep ready. Working with one portion of the dough at a time, using your fingers press out a 3-inch patty. Brush the top surface lightly with water and place one portion of the dal filling in the center. Lift the edges over the filling, bring them together and pinch to secure. Next, softly push in the pinched edges down to make a slight depression in the center and to flatten the patty to 1-inch thick. Brush the

entire kachauri lightly with the flour-water paste and save for later. Finish assembling all the kachauries. Cover with a clean, damp cotton kitchen towel and set aside.

6. Heat the oil in a wok or skillet using moderate to high heat until it achieves 300°F to 325°F on a frying thermometer, or when a small piece of the dough dropped into the hot oil surges to the surface of the oil after fifteen to 20 seconds. Reduce the heat to medium and put in the kachauries, adding as many as the wok can hold simultaneously without crowding, and fry slowly, turning only once after the bottom is golden-brown, approximately 3 to four minutes. When the other side is golden-brown, approximately 3 to four minutes more, remove from the wok with a slotted metal spatula and move to paper towels to drain. Serve instantly, or allow to cool down and place in your fridge for a maximum of half a month.

PATTY 1: MUSHROOM TURNOVERS

This recipe is called "Mushroom Patty" in Hindi

Yield: 24 pieces

"Patties" are super cheap, and highly popular among kids in India. These were practically the only food available in my school canteen back in the day.

Ingredients:

- ¼ cup finely chopped fresh cilantro, including soft stems
- ½ teaspoon salt, or to taste
- 1 (20-ounce) package frozen puff pastry sheets (2 sheets)
- 1 large egg white, beaten lightly with 1 tablespoon water
- 1 large onion, finely chopped
- 1 teaspoon minced fresh garlic
- 1 to 3 green chile peppers, such as serrano, minced with seeds
- 1½ to 2 teaspoons Basic Curry Powder (Homemade or store-bought)
- 2 tablespoons vegetable oil
- 3 cups finely chopped mushrooms
- 3 tablespoons all-purpose flour

Directions:

1. Ready the curry powder. Heat the oil in a big non-stick wok or saucepan using moderate to high heat and cook the onion, stirring, until transparent, approximately two to three minutes. Put in the garlic, green chile peppers, curry powder, and flour, and stir using moderate to low heat until the garlic and onion are golden, approximately two to three minutes. Put in the mushrooms, cilantro, and salt and cook until the mixture is completely dry, another three to five minutes. Allow to cool before using.
2. Divide the filling into two equal parts, one for each pastry sheet. Thaw the pastry sheets at room temperature, until they become a little tender but still cold to the touch, fifteen to twenty minutes.
3. Preheat your oven to 375°F. Lightly grease a baking sheet. On a mildly floured surface, working with each pastry sheet separately, unfold and softly roll it with a rolling pin to make it smooth. Next, cut each sheet into 12 squares. Roll each square to make it a little bigger. Moisten the edges with water, place 1 tablespoon of filling in the center of each square and fold one corner over the filling to the diagonal corner to form a triangle. Seal the edges by pressing with the back of a fork.
4. Brush the top of each turnover with the beaten egg and then poke a few holes with a fork so the steam can escape. Put the turnovers on the baking sheet and bake until puffed and golden, approximately twenty minutes. Move to cooling racks. Serve hot or at room temperature.

PATTY 2: CURRIED CHICKEN OR LAMB TURNOVERS

This recipe is called "Chicken/Mutton patty" in Hindi

Yield: 24 pieces

Ingredients:

- ¼ teaspoon ground turmeric
- ½ cup finely chopped fresh cilantro, including soft stems
- ½ teaspoon garam masala
- ½ teaspoon salt, or to taste

- 1 (20-ounce) package frozen puff pastry sheets (2 sheets)
- 1 large egg white, beaten lightly with 1 tablespoon water
- 1 large onion, finely chopped
- 1 pound ground chicken or lamb
- 1 tablespoon ground coriander
- 1 teaspoon dried fenugreek leaves
- 1 teaspoon ground cumin
- 1 to 3 fresh green chile peppers, such as serrano, minced with seeds
- 2 tablespoons all-purpose flour

Directions:

1. Put everything (except the flour, puff pastry, and the egg wash) in a big non-stick skillet or saucepan and cook using moderate to high heat, stirring and breaking up any lumps in the ground chicken, until a golden colour is achieved, approximately five minutes. If using lamb, cook an extra 5 to seven minutes. Reserve the pan.
2. Let the meat cool until it is safe sufficient to handle, approximately fifteen minutes, then move to a food processor, put in the flour, and process to make it as smooth as possible. Return to the pan and cook approximately five minutes to bind the filling and remove the raw taste of the flour.
3. Divide the filling into two equal parts, one for each pastry sheet. Thaw the pastry sheets at room temperature, until they become a little tender but still cold to the touch, fifteen to twenty minutes.
4. Preheat your oven to 375°F. Lightly grease a baking sheet. On a mildly floured surface, working with each pastry sheet separately, unfold and softly roll it with a rolling pin to make it smooth. Next, cut each sheet into 12 squares. Roll each square to make it a little bigger. Moisten the edges with water, place 1 tablespoon of filling in the center of each square and fold one corner over the filling to the diagonal corner to form a triangle. Seal the edges by pressing with the back of a fork.
5. Brush the top of each turnover with the beaten egg and then poke a few holes with a fork so the steam can escape. Put the turnovers on the baking sheet and bake until puffed and golden, approximately twenty minutes. Move to cooling racks. Serve hot or at room temperature.

PUFF PASTRY ROLLS

This recipe is called "Puff pastry ke rolls" in Hindi

Yield: 24 pieces

Ingredients:

- ¼ cup finely chopped fresh cilantro, including soft stems
- 1 (20-ounce) package frozen puff pastry sheets (2 sheets)
- 2 teaspoons Chaat Masala (Homemade or store-bought)
- 2 to 3 scallions, green parts only, minced
- 24 thick asparagus spears, each approximately 6 inches long

Directions:

1. Ready the chaat masala. Thaw the pastry sheets at room temperature until they become a little tender but still cold to the touch, fifteen to twenty minutes. Preheat your oven to 350°F and mildly grease a baking sheet.
2. On a mildly floured surface, unfold and sprinkle both the pastry sheets uniformly with the chaat masala, scallion, and cilantro and gently, use a rolling pin to roll each sheet, ensuring that the scallion and cilantro are pressed well into the pastry. (Drizzle with dry flour if the dough starts to become gluey.) Next, cut each sheet into 12 squares. Roll each square to make it a little bigger.
3. Working with each square separately, place one asparagus spear along the diagonal across the center with approximately 1 inch of the tip outside the pastry. Fold in half over the asparagus, then make a roll. Moisten the corner with water and press to secure. Place, 1-inch apart, on the baking sheet, with the sealed side down. Bake until crunchy and golden, fifteen to twenty minutes. Move to cooling racks. Serve hot or at room temperature.

PUFF PASTRY WITH AJWAIN SEEDS

This recipe is version of a dish commonly referred to as "Ajwain ki puff pastry" in India

Yield: 30 pieces

A popular, cheap, and insanely delicious snack commonly available I pretty much every bakery in India.

Ingredients:

- ¼ to ⅓ teaspoon crudely ground ajwain seeds
- ½ teaspoon cumin seeds, dry-roasted and crudely ground (See the dry-roasting section in Introduction)
- 1 large egg white
- 1 tablespoon all-purpose flour for dusting
- 1 tablespoon water
- Half of 1 (20-ounce) package frozen puff pastry (1 sheet)

Directions:

1. Ready the cumin seeds. Preheat your oven to 325°F. Thaw the pastry sheet at room temperature, until it is slightly softened but still cold to the touch, fifteen to twenty minutes. Lightly grease a baking sheet. On a mildly floured surface, unfold and softly roll the pastry sheet to make a smooth 14-inch square. Cut in half.
2. In a small-sized container, whisk together the egg white and water and brush it lightly over each half sheet. Sprinkle the cumin and ajwain seeds uniformly on one half, then place the second half over it, egg wash side down. Dust lightly with flour and roll softly with a rolling pin to make a 14-by-7-inch rectangle (or larger).
3. Cut across the diagonal into approximately 30 half-inch strips. Twist and lightly stretch each strip and place, approximately 1 inch apart, on a mildly greased baking sheet. Brush with the egg wash for a shiny glaze and bake until crunchy and golden, approximately ten to twelve minutes. Serve hot or at room temperature.

RED BELL PEPPER-POTATO PASTRY SWIRLS

This recipe is called "Shimla mirch aur aalu ki Matthi" in Hindi

Yield: 48 pieces

A great snack if guests are coming over! Takes a while to prepare, but it is totally worth it.

Ingredients:

- ¼ teaspoon salt, or to taste
- ½ teaspoon garam masala
- ½ teaspoon ground cumin
- 1 (20-ounce) package frozen puff pastry sheets (2 sheets)
- 1 medium onion, crudely chopped
- 1 tablespoon vegetable oil
- 1½ tablespoons ground coriander
- 2 tablespoons peeled and minced fresh ginger
- 3 large russet (or any) potatoes
- 3 red bell peppers

Directions:

1. Preheat the broiler and mildly grease a broiler-safe baking sheet. Thaw the pastry sheets at room temperature, until they become a little tender but still cold to the touch, fifteen to twenty minutes In the meantime, cook the potatoes in lightly salted boiling water to cover until soft, approximately twenty minutes, then peel and mash them.
2. Slice the bell peppers in half and place them, cut side down, on the baking sheet, place on the top rack of the oven or under the broiler, and broil the peppers until thoroughly charred, approximately five minutes. Take out of the oven, and reduce the oven heat to 325°F. Move the peppers to a container, then cover with a dish or a seal within a zip-closure plastic bag until cool sufficient to handle. Next, peel off and discard most of the charred skin, leaving some on for flavour. Slice thinly.
3. Heat the oil in a big non-stick wok or saucepan using moderate to high heat and cook the onion, stirring, until a golden colour is achieved, approximately two minutes. Stir in the ginger and cook another minute. Put in the mashed potatoes, coriander, cumin, garam masala, and salt, and cook stirring until a golden colour is achieved, approximately two to three minutes. Stir in the roasted bell peppers and stir approximately two minutes to blend the flavours. Allow to cool to room temperature, then split into 2 equal parts.
4. On a mildly floured surface, working with each pastry sheet separately, unfold and softly roll the sheet to make it smooth. Placing the shorter side toward you and spread one half of the potato filling uniformly over the sheet, leaving approximately a 3/4-inch border along the edges. Moisten the border with water.
5. Starting from the side closest to you, roll firmly like a jelly roll. When you reach the end, push softly on the moistened edge to secure the roll. Lightly roll back

and forth to make the roll longer. Keeping the sealed side down, slice into 24 ½-inch swirls and place them 1 inch apart on a baking sheet. Replicate the process for the second pastry sheet. Bake until crunchy and golden, approximately fifteen to twenty minutes. Serve hot or at room temperature.

SALTY FINGER PASTRIES Ⓥ

This recipe is called "Namak-paarae or nimki" in Hindi

Yield: 4 to 6 servings

Ingredients:

- ½ teaspoon crudely ground ajwain seeds
- ½ teaspoon salt, or to taste
- ½ to 2 cups peanut oil for deep-frying
- 1 tablespoon cornstarch
- 1½ cups self-rising flour, plus more for dusting
- 3 tablespoons vegetable oil
- About ⅓ cup water

Directions:

1. Put the flour, cornstarch, oil, ajwain seeds, and salt into a food processor and pulse a few times to mix. Next, with the motor running, slowly and gradually pour in water and process until the dough gathers into a semi-firm ball that does not stick to the sides of the work container. Move to a container, cover, and set aside 1 to four hours. This allows the gluten to develop.
2. Slightly oil your clean hands and gather the dough into a smooth, large ball. Coat it well with the dry flour, use your hands and fingers to compress it into a disc, and roll it into a large 8- to 9-inch circle (don't worry approximately the shape) approximately ⅛ inch thick. If the dough sticks to the rolling surface, dust with more flour. (The rolling can be done on a mildly floured surface, but this is not a common practice in India.)
3. Using a knife, make diagonal cuts through the length of the rolled circle, approximately ½ inch apart. Next, make opposite diagonal cuts, separating the rolled dough into diamond-shaped bits.

4. Heat the oil in a big wok or over moderate heat until it reaches 300°F to 325°F on a frying thermometer, or when a small drop of dough begins to bubble while it is still immersed. (Reduce the heat if it rises instantly or browns.) Put in the dough bits, as many as the wok can comfortably hold simultaneously, and fry, turning as required with a slotted spatula until crunchy and appears mildly golden. Do not brown them and ensure that the centers are crisp. (Check by breaking one piece.) Move with a slotted spatula to paper towel to drain. Allow to cool completely, then store in airtight containers at room temperature, up to sixty days.

SAMOSA

Samosas are basically stuffed fried pastries, most commonly triangular in shape. The cheapest and most common stuffing you will find all across India is spicy mashed potato, but the possibilities are endless. You will find a few of the most popular samosa stuffing recipes under the next heading.

Samosas commonly enjoyed with chutneys, so feel free to randomly pick out any chutney from the chutney section to try with a samosa you prepare.

BASIC SAMOSA Ⓥ

This recipe is called "Samosa" in Hindi

Yield: 24 pieces

The basic most commonly available triangular samosa. Use the potato filling with this if you want to enjoy the most popular samosa Indian samosa!

Ingredients:

- ½ teaspoon crudely ground ajwain seeds
- ½ teaspoon salt, or to taste

- 1 cup all-purpose flour in a moderate-sized container or a pie dish, for coating and dusting
- 1 recipe any Samosa Filling
- 1½ cups self-rising flour
- 1½ to 2 cups peanut oil for deep-frying
- 3 tablespoons vegetable oil
- About ⅓ cup water

Directions:

1. Ready the filling. Next, ready the dough: Put the self-rising flour, oil, ajwain seeds, and salt into a food processor and pulse until blended. While the motor runs, slowly and gradually pour in water and process until the flour gathers into a semi-firm ball that does not stick to the sides of the work container. Move to a container, cover using plastic wrap or a lid, and let rest at least 1 hour and up to four hours. (This lets the gluten develop.) If keeping for a longer period, place the dough in your fridge.

2. To roll and assemble: Slightly oil your clean hands (to stop the dough from sticking to them), then split into 12 1½-inch balls. Cover using aluminium foil and save for later. Work with each ball one at a time, and use your hands and fingers to compress it into a disc, cover thoroughly with dry flour, then roll using a rolling pin into a 6- to 7-inch circle of uniform ⅛-inch thickness. Use more dry flour as needed if the dough becomes sticky again.

3. Slice the circle in half and brush with water approximately ½-inch in, along the straight edge. Pick up the two corners and place one over and around the other along the straight edge, then push along the straight edge to secure, making a cone. Finally, pinch the peak of the cone to secure.

4. Another way is to fold in half, sealing the straight edge to make a simpler cone.

5. Hold the cone vertically such that the open end is on top. Fill the mouth of the cone with 2 to 3 tablespoons of filling. Brush the edges of the mouth of the cone with water and push them together to secure. You should have a stuffed triangular pastry when you're done. Cover with foil and allow to sit until ready to fry. Replicate the process for all the other balls of dough.

6. To fry: Heat the oil in a wok or skillet using moderate to high heat until it achieves 325°F to 350°F on a frying thermometer, or when a small piece of the dough dropped into the hot oil surges to the surface of the oil after fifteen to 20 seconds. Put the samosas in the wok, as many as it can hold simultaneously without crowding, and fry, turning them a few times with a slotted spatula, until crunchy and golden on all sides, about four to five minutes. (If the

samosas brown too swiftly, it means the heat is too high; lower it.) Move to paper towels to drain, then serve.

SEVEN LAYERS SAMOSA

This recipe is called "Satpura samosae" in Hindi

Yield: 16 pieces

Ingredients:

- ⅛ teaspoon ground asafoetida
- ¼ teaspoon cayenne pepper, or to taste
- ¼ teaspoon salt, or to taste
- ¼ to ⅓ cup melted unsalted butter or vegetable oil
- ½ teaspoon garam masala
- 1 large russet (or any) potato
- 1 tablespoon melted ghee or vegetable oil
- 1 teaspoon cumin seeds
- 7 phyllo pastry sheets (about ¼ pound)

Directions:

1. Boil the potato in lightly salted water to cover until tender, approximately twenty minutes. Drain, allow to cool down, then peel and mash in a small-sized container. Heat the oil in a small-sized non-stick wok or saucepan using moderate to high heat and put in the cumin seeds; they should sizzle when they touch the hot oil. Swiftly put in the mashed potato, garam masala, cayenne pepper, asafoetida, and salt, and stir until a golden colour is achieved, approximately five to seven minutes. Allow to cool.

2. Moisten each phyllo sheet generously with the melted butter and stack one on top of the other on a cutting board. Using a sharp knife, cut along the length into 4 equal strips, approximately 3 inches wide, cutting through all 7 sheets. Cut each strip in half along the diagonal and then cut each half in half again to make a total of 16 rectangles, each made up of 7 layers. Cover with a damp (not wet) sanitized kitchen towel.

3. Preheat your oven to 350°F. Lightly grease a baking sheet. Using a rolling pin, lightly roll each rectangular stack of 7 layers to ensure the layers adhere to

each other properly. Brush the top layer with butter and place 1 teaspoon of the filling in the center. Fold in half to, cover the filling. Press the edges well to secure in the filling. Replicate the process for the remain-ing rectangles.

4. Brush the top and bottom layers of the samosas generously with butter once again and place on the baking sheet. Bake until crunchy and golden, fifteen to twenty minutes. Move to cooling racks. Serve.

SINDHI-STYLE SAMOSA Ⓥ

This recipe is called "Sindhi samosae" in Hindi

Yield: 24 pieces

Sindh is now a part of Pakistan, but the Sindhi people and their cuisines are very much a part of India!

Ingredients:

- ¼ teaspoon salt, or to taste
- 1 cup all-purpose flour in a moderate-sized container or a pie dish, for coating and dusting
- 1 recipe any Samosa Filling of your choice
- 1½ cups self-rising flour
- 1½ teaspoons fennel seeds, crudely ground
- 2 to 3 cups peanut oil for deep-frying
- About ¾ cup water

Directions:

1. Ready the filling. Next, in a small-sized container, combine 2 tablespoons of the self-rising flour with approximately 2 tablespoons water to make a thick paste that will be used as a glue for sealing the pastries.

2. Ready the dough: Put the rest of the self-rising flour, fennel seeds, and salt into a food processor and pulse until blended. While the motor runs, slowly and gradually pour in water and process until the flour gathers into a pliable ball that does not stick to the sides of the work container. (This dough does not need to rest.)

3. To roll and assemble: Split the dough into 8 balls. Flatten each one into a 3- to 4-inch disc. Working with 4 discs at a time, brush the top surface of each thoroughly with oil then dust each one with approximately 2 teaspoons flour. Working with the rest of the 4 discs one at a time, brush with oil and place on top of one of the floured discs, oil side down, like a sandwich. Next, press each "sandwich" together to make one big disc. You will now have four large discs.

4. Working with each of the 4 discs one at a time, sprinkle mildly with the flour and roll using a rolling pin to make 8- to 9-inch circles of uniform ⅛-inch thickness. (Use more dry flour as needed if the dough becomes sticky again.)

5. Heat a griddle or a skillet over moderate heat and cook each rolled circle very lightly on both sides until it just begins to firm up but not brown, approximately half a minute per side. (You'll see the edges of the sandwiched circle starting to separate.) Transfer it to a cutting board. Cautiously pull the two sides apart to split into two paper-thin circles, and stack them. Replicate the process for the other three discs. When you're done, you should have a stack of 8 samosa skins. Slice the stack of skins into 3 equal parts, making a total of 24 long strips. Keep covered with foil.

6. Working with each strip separately, lay it along the length in front of you on the work surface and place approximately 1 tablespoon of the filling on the strip near the lower right corner. Next, fold the right corner over the filling to the left side to make a triangle. Repeatedly fold the stuffed triangle along the diagonal from one side to the other until you get to the end of the dough strip. Tuck in any spare dough to secure. When you're done, you should have a multi-folded triangle. Replicate the process for all the strips.

7. Heat the oil in a wok or skillet using moderate to high heat until it achieves 325°F to 350°F on a frying thermometer or when a small piece of dough dropped into the hot oil surges to the surface of the oil after fifteen to 20 seconds. Add as many samosas as the wok can hold simultaneously without crowding, and fry, turning them a few times with a slotted spatula, until crunchy and golden on all sides, about four to five minutes. (If the samosas brown too swiftly, lower the heat.) Move to paper towels to drain, then serve.

STUFFED PHYLLO BAKED SAMOSA

This recipe is called "Potli-samosae" in Hindi

Yield: 24 pieces

Ingredients:

- ¼ to ⅓ cup melted unsalted butter or vegetable oil
- 1 recipe any <u>Samosa Filling</u> of your choice
- 12 phyllo pastry sheets (about ½ pound)

Directions:

1. Brush each phyllo sheet liberally with butter and stack one on top of the other on a cutting board. Using a sharp knife, cut the sheets in half, along the diagonal, to make a total of 24 pieces. Stack once again, and cover with a damp (not wet) sanitized kitchen towel.
2. Preheat your oven to 350°F. Lightly grease a mini-muffin pan or a baking sheet. Working with each piece separately, fold in half and then in half again to make an approximately 6-by-4-inch rectangle. Put approximately 1 tablespoon of the filling in the center, then pick up the phyllo by the four corners and pinch them together just above the filling to secure, making a little pouch.
3. Another way is to tie each one lightly with chives, scallion greens, or thin strips of carrots, or any other greens or vegetables. Replicate the process for all the pieces.
4. Brush all the pouches with the butter, and place each in one cup of the muffin pan or all of them on a baking sheet and bake until crunchy and golden, approximately 25 minutes. Move to cooling racks. Serve hot, warm, or at room temperature.

STUFFED PHYLLO SAMOSA

This recipe is called "Phyllo Ke samosae" in Hindi

Yield: 24 pieces

Ingredients:

- 1 recipe any <u>Samosa Filling</u> of your choice
- 1 to 2 tablespoons melted butter or vegetable oil
- 6 phyllo pastry sheets (about ¼ pound)

Directions:

1. Brush each phyllo sheet with melted butter and stack one on top of the other on a cutting board. Using a sharp knife, cut them along the length into 4 equal strips, each approximately 3 inches wide. You should have 24 long strips. Stack again and cover with a damp (not wet) sanitized kitchen towel.

2. Preheat your oven to 350°F. Lightly grease a baking sheet. Working with each strip separately, place it along the length in front of you on the work surface and put approximately 1 tablespoon of the filling near the lower right corner. Fold the right corner over the filling to the left side to make a triangle. Repeatedly fold the stuffed triangle along the diagonal from one side to the other until you get to the end of the phyllo. Tuck in any extra to secure. When you're done, you should have a multifolded triangle. Replicate the process for all the strips.

3. Brush the top of all the triangles with the butter, place them on the baking sheet, and bake, flipping over once midway through baking, until crunchy and golden, approximately 25 minutes. Move to cooling racks. Serve hot, warm, or at room temperature.

TORTILLA SAMOSA Ⓥ

This recipe is called "Tortilla samosa" in Hindi

Yield: 24 pieces

A delicious combo of an Indian and Mexican snack!

Ingredients:

- 1 recipe any <u>Samosa Filling</u> of your choice
- 1½ to 2 cups peanut oil for deep-frying
- 12 (8- to 9-inch) flour tortillas

Directions:

1. 1. Stack and cut the tortillas in half to make 24 semicircles. Working with each half separately, brush with water approximately ½-inch in, along all the edges. Next, place 1½ to 2 tablespoons of the samosa filling on one side of the semi circle. Fold the other side over the filling to cover it. Press the edges well to secure in the filling. Replicate the process for the rest of the halves.

2. To roll and assemble: Slightly oil your clean hands (to stop the dough from sticking to them), then split into 12 1½-inch balls. Cover using aluminium foil and save for later. Work with each ball one at a time, and use your hands and fingers to compress it into a disc, cover thoroughly with dry flour, then roll using a rolling pin into a 6- to 7-inch circle of uniform ⅛-inch thickness. Use more dry flour as needed if the dough becomes sticky again.

3. Slice the circle in half and brush with water approximately ½-inch in, along the straight edge. Pick up the two corners and place one over and around the other along the straight edge, then push along the straight edge to secure, making a cone. Finally, pinch the peak of the cone to secure.

4. Another way is to fold in half, sealing the straight edge to make a simpler cone.

5. Hold the cone vertically such that the open end is on top. Fill the mouth of the cone with 2 to 3 tablespoons of filling. Brush the edges of the mouth of the cone with water and push them together to secure. You should have a stuffed triangular pastry when you're done. Cover with foil and allow to sit until ready to fry. Replicate the process for all the other balls of dough.

6. To fry: Heat the oil in a wok or skillet using moderate to high heat until it achieves 325°F to 350°F on a frying thermometer, or when a small piece of the dough dropped into the hot oil surges to the surface of the oil after fifteen to 20 seconds. Put the samosas in the wok, as many as it can hold simultaneously without crowding, and fry, turning them a few times with a slotted spatula, until crunchy and golden on all sides, about four to five minutes. (If the samosas brown too swiftly, it means the heat is too high; lower it.) Move to paper towels to drain, then serve.

FILLINGS FOR SAMOSAS

BASIC POTATO FILLING Ⓥ

This recipe is called "Samosae ka aalu ka masala" in Hindi

Yield: Approximately 4 cups

The most common Samosa filling you will find in India!

Ingredients:

- ¼ cup finely chopped fresh cilantro, including soft stems
- ½ teaspoon crudely ground fenugreek seeds
- ½ teaspoon garam masala
- ½ teaspoon salt, or to taste
- 1 teaspoon mango powder
- 1 to 3 fresh green chile peppers, such as serrano, minced with seeds
- 1½ tablespoons ground coriander
- 2 tablespoons peanut oil
- 2 tablespoons peeled and minced fresh ginger
- 2 teaspoons cumin seeds
- 4 to 5 medium russet (or any) potatoes (about 1½ pounds)

Directions:

1. Cook the potatoes in lightly salted boiling water to cover until tender, approximately twenty minutes. Drain, allow to cool down, then peel and finely chop. Heat the oil in a big non-stick wok or saucepan using moderate to high heat and put in the cumin seeds; they should sizzle when they touch the hot oil. Swiftly put in the fenugreek seeds and stir in the potatoes.
2. Stir approximately two minutes, then Put in the ginger, green chile peppers, coriander, salt, and garam masala, and stir occasionally until the potatoes are golden, approximately ten minutes.
3. Put in the cilantro and mango powder and cook another 5 minutes. Turn off the heat and allow to cool down before using.

GREEN PEA FILLING Ⓥ

This recipe is called "Samosae ka matar ka masala" in Hindi

Yield: Approximately 4 cups

Green peas are delicious and nutritious!

Ingredients:

- ⅛ teaspoon ground asafoetida
- ½ teaspoon cayenne pepper, or to taste
- ½ teaspoon salt, or to taste
- 1 cup water
- 1 large onion, finely chopped
- 1 teaspoon ground fennel seeds
- 1 teaspoon ground ginger
- 1¼ cups green split peas (muttar dal), sorted and washed in 3 to 4 changes of water
- 1½ teaspoons cumin seeds
- 2 tablespoons vegetable oil
- 2 teaspoons ground coriander
- 2 teaspoons mango powder

Directions:

1. Immerse the split peas overnight in water to cover by 2 inches, then drain. Heat the oil in a small-sized non-stick wok or saucepan using moderate to high heat and put in the cumin seeds; they should sizzle when they touch the hot oil. Swiftly put in the onion and cook, stirring, until a golden colour is achieved, approximately two minutes.
2. Put in the dal, coriander, ginger, fennel seeds, cayenne pepper, salt, and asafoetida, and cook approximately one minute. Put in the water, bring to a quick boil using high heat, then reduce the heat to low, cover the pan and cook until the split peas become soft, approximately ten minutes. Stir in the mango powder and allow to cool down before using.

MEAT FILLING

This recipe is called "Samosae ka gosht ka masala" in Hindi

Yield: Approximately 3 cups

Feel free to use any kind of meat!

Ingredients:

- ¼ teaspoon freshly ground nutmeg

- ¼ teaspoon ground turmeric
- ½ cup bread crumbs
- ½ teaspoon cayenne pepper, or to taste
- ½ teaspoon salt, or to taste
- 1 cup crudely chopped fresh cilantro, including soft stems
- 1 cup fresh fenugreek leaves
- 1 cup frozen peas, thawed
- 1 fresh green chile pepper, such as serrano, crudely chopped
- 1 pound extra lean ground meat (lamb, beef, or chicken)
- 1 tablespoon garam masala
- 2 large cloves fresh garlic, peeled
- 5 to 7 quarter-size slices peeled fresh ginger

Directions:

1. Using a food processor, combine and pulse the fenugreek leaves, cilantro, garlic, ginger, and green chile pepper until minced. Add all the rest of the ingredients, except the peas, and process once more to mix thoroughly.
2. Move to a large non-stick wok or skillet, stir in the peas, and cook, stirring, using moderate to high heat until the meat is golden and completely dry, approximately eight to ten minutes. Allow to cool before using.

MOONG DAL FILLING Ⓥ

This recipe is called "Samosae ka mung dal ka Masala" in Hindi

Yield: Approximately 4 cups

Mung dal beans make a great filling for the samosa!

Ingredients:

- ¼ teaspoon ground turmeric
- ½ teaspoon salt, or to taste
- 1 cup finely chopped fresh spinach
- 1 cup water
- 1 fresh green chile pepper, such as serrano, minced with seeds
- 1 tablespoon ground coriander

- 1 teaspoon cumin seeds
- 1¼ cup dried yellow mung beans (dhulli mung dal), sorted and washed in 3 to 4 changes of water
- 1½ tablespoons peeled and minced fresh ginger
- 2 tablespoons vegetable oil

Directions:

1. Immerse the mung beans overnight in water to cover by 2 inches, then drain. Heat the oil in a big non-stick wok or saucepan using moderate to high heat and put in the cumin seeds; they should sizzle when they touch the hot oil. Swiftly put in the ginger, green chile pepper, and coriander, and stir for approximately half a minute.
2. Put in the spinach and stir until wilted, approximately one minute. Stir in the mung beans, turmeric, and salt, and stir approximately two minutes. Put in the water, reduce the heat to moderate to low, cover the pan and cook until all the water has been absorbed and the dal is soft, approximately ten minutes. Allow to cool before using.

SPROUTED GREEN MUNG BEAN FILLING

Ⓥ

This recipe is called "Samosae ka phooti mung dal ka masala" in Hindi

Yield: Approximately 4 cups

Ingredients:

- ½ cup finely chopped fresh cilantro, including soft stems
- ½ teaspoon ground turmeric
- 1 large onion, finely chopped
- 1 teaspoon salt, or to taste
- 1 to 3 fresh green chile pepper, such as serrano, minced with seeds
- 2 cups sprouted green mung beans (Sprout your own as shown in the "Indian Cooking 101" section, or buy in a store)
- 2 tablespoons fresh lemon juice
- 2 tablespoons ground coriander

- 2 tablespoons peanut oil
- 2 teaspoons cumin seeds
- 6 small russet (or any) potatoes

Directions:

1. Ready the mung beans in advance. Cook the potatoes in lightly salted boiling water to cover until tender, approximately twenty minutes. Drain, allow to cool down, then grate into a moderate-sized container.
2. Heat the oil in a big non-stick wok or saucepan using moderate to high heat and put in the cumin seeds; they should sizzle when they touch the hot oil. Swiftly put in the onions and cook, stirring, until a golden colour is achieved, approximately five minutes.
3. Put in the coriander and turmeric, then stir in the green chiles, sprouted dal, and salt, and cook approximately three minutes. Put in the grated potatoes, lemon juice, and cilantro, and cook using moderate to high heat, stirring, until completely dry, approximately five minutes. Turn off the heat and allow to cool down before using.

VEGETABLE FILLING Ⓥ

This recipe is called "Samosae ka sabziyon ka masala" in Hindi

Yield: Approximately 4 cups

Feel free to use vegetables of your choice! You don't have to follow the recipe exactly. Invent a samosa tailored exactly to your taste!

Ingredients:

- ½ teaspoon salt, or to taste
- 1 medium onion, finely chopped
- 1 tablespoon peeled and finely chopped fresh ginger
- 1 to 3 fresh green chile peppers, such as serrano, minced with seeds
- 1½ to 2 tablespoons Spicy Masala for Wok-Cooked Foods (Kadhai Masala), or store-bought
- 2 tablespoons vegetable oil
- 4 cups finely chopped mixed fresh or frozen vegetables

- Freshly ground black pepper, to taste

Directions:

1. Ready the kadaai masala. Heat the oil in a big non-stick wok or saucepan using moderate to high heat and put in the kadhai masala; it should sizzle when they touch the hot oil. Swiftly put in the onion and stir approximately two minutes.
2. Put in the green chile peppers, ginger, vegetables, salt, and black pepper, and cook over moderate heat the first two to three minutes, and then using moderate to low heat until the vegetables are soft, 5 to 7 min-utes more. Turn off the heat and allow to cool down before using.

FRITTERS (PAKORAE)

These fried treats are the first things that come to mind on a rainy day in North India. There are probably a million kinds of pakodas eaten in India as the combinations of batters and what you put in the batter are endless. These are almost always served with a chutney and served immediately after being taken out of the wok.

Even though the possibilities are endless, the most commonly used batter is chickpea flour (called "besan" in Hindi). The batter needs to be the right thickness, and that is something you will know after practice. If the batter is too thin, it won't stick to the stuff you're covering with it, and if you make it too thick, the pakora will taste a little too heavy doughy. You can do this by adjusting the amount of water. Also, it is important to sift to batter to make sure all the lumps are eliminated, and the flour stays nice and fluffy.

If you have guests coming over and you wish to pre-prepare your pakoras, it is a good idea to double fry them. Lightly fry the pakoras in advance and store in your fridge in an air-tight container. These will keep in the fridge for about five to six days. When it is time to serve, take them out of the fridge, bring them to room temperature, and refry in hot oil. If the oil, or the pakoras aren't hot enough, the pakoras will absorb more oil than they need to.

FRYING FRITTERS

This technique is called "Pakorae Talna" in Hindi

This technique will be used in all the pakora recipes that follow, so you might want to bookmark this.

Directions:

1. Heat the oil in a wok or skillet until it reaches 350°F to 375°F on a frying thermometer or a small teaspoon of batter dropped into the hot oil bubbles and surges to the surface of the oil instantly.
2. With clean hands, put the chopped or chopped vegetables (or other items) into the batter (in batches if needed) and mix lightly using your fingers. Work with each piece one at a time and shake off the surplus batter by tapping it lightly against the sides of the batter container, then put it into the hot oil cautiously using your fingers (or with tongs) to avoid oil spluttering. Add as many pieces as the wok can hold simultaneously without crowding, and fry each batch, turning a few times with a slotted spoon, until crunchy and golden on all sides, approximately one to two minutes for small, thin pieces, approximately two to three minutes for bigger pieces. Move to paper towels to drain. Repeat the process with rest of the pieces.

BASIC BATTER FOR PAKORA Ⓥ

This recipe is called "Pakorae ka besan" in Hindi

Yield: 40 to 50 fritters

This is the most basic batter for pakora fritters, to which you can add as many or as few herbs and spices as you wish. With no other additions, this basic recipe forms a light, crisp coating around a large array of foods. More than anything else, it is the consistency of the batter that is really important. Thick, it will be doughy, thin it will not coat properly.

Ingredients:

- ⅛ teaspoon baking soda

- ⅓ teaspoon salt, or to taste
- ⅓ to ½ cup water
- ½ cup chickpea flour (besan)

Directions:

1. Sieve the chickpea flour into a moderate-sized container, put in the salt and baking soda and mix thoroughly.
2. Add ⅓ cup water to make a smooth batter of medium consistency. If the batter is thin, add some more chickpea flour; if it appears too thick, stir in some more water. The batter is now ready.

SLICED, CHOPPED, AND STUFFED VEGETABLE FRITTERS

BELL PEPPER FRITTERS Ⓥ

This recipe is called "Shimla mirch kae pakorae" in Hindi

Yield: Approximately 30 pieces

Ingredients:

- ½ teaspoon crudely ground ajwain seeds
- ½ teaspoon Chaat Masala (Homemade or store-bought)
- ½ teaspoon hot red pepper flakes, or to taste
- 1 recipe Basic Batter for Pakora Fritters
- 1 tablespoon Basic Ginger Paste (Homemade or store-bought)
- 1½ to 2 cups oil for deep-frying
- 2 teaspoons ground coriander
- 3 to 4 orange or red bell peppers, stemmed and seeded

Directions:

1. Ready the ginger-garlic paste and chaat masala. Cut each bell pepper along the length into 2 halves, then cross-wise into ½-inch thick half moons.
2. Ready the basic batter. Stir in the coriander, ajwain seeds, red pepper flakes, and ginger-garlic paste.
3. Put in the bell pepper slices to the batter. Heat the oil and fry the bell pepper slices as per directions under the "Frying Fritters" heading at the start of this section. Move all the fried pakoras to a serving platter, sprinkle the chaat masala on top, and serve.

CABBAGE ROLL FRITTERS Ⓥ

This recipe is called "Bundh gobhi kae pakorae" in Hindi

Yield: twelve to fifteen pieces

Ingredients:

- ½ teaspoon Chaat Masala (Homemade or store-bought)
- 1 recipe Basic Batter for Pakora Fritters
- 1½ cup any dry-cooked vegetable or meat filling (choose from Fillings for Samosa Pastries)
- 1½ to 2 cups oil for deep-frying
- Shredded cabbage to line a platter
- twelve to fifteen outer leaves Napa cabbage

Directions:

1. Ready the chaat masala and the filling, then ready the batter. Rinse and cut off the leafy top 5 inches of each cabbage leaf. Put in a microwave-safe dish, cover with the lid of the dish, and cook 3 to four minutes on high power, to wilt the leaves. (Or wilt over moderate heat in a big pan.) Allow to cool.
2. Put approximately 2 tablespoons or more of the filling on each leaf, along the diagonal at the stem end, folding it with the stem end tucked inside, to make a roll. Pinch the edges to secure the roll. Dip each roll in the batter to coat it well.
3. Fry using the directions under "Frying Fritters" at the start of this section. Move all the fried pakoras to a serving platter, sprinkle the chaat masala on top, and serve on a bed of shredded cabbage.

CAULIFLOWER FRITTERS Ⓥ

This recipe is called "Gobhi kae pakorae" in Hindi

Yield: 20 to 25 pieces

Ingredients:

- ¼ cup minced fresh cilantro, including soft stems
- ¼ cup mustard oil for deep-frying
- ¼ teaspoon garam masala
- ½ teaspoon crudely ground ajwain seeds
- ½ teaspoon hot red pepper flakes, or to taste
- ½ teaspoon salt, or to taste
- 1 large head cauliflower (about 1½ pounds), cut into 2-inch florets
- 1 teaspoon Chaat Masala (Homemade or store-bought)
- 1 to 2 tablespoons chickpea flour
- 1 to 3 fresh green chile peppers, such as serrano, minced with seeds
- 1½ recipes Basic Batter for Pakora Fritters
- 1½ to 2 cups peanut oil for deep-frying

Directions:

1. Ready the chaat masala. Put the cauliflower florets in a container and toss with salt and red pepper flakes. Set aside to let the flavours blend. Ready the basic batter. Stir in the chickpea flour, cilantro, green chile peppers, garam masala, and ajwain seeds. Put in the florets to the batter. Fry using the directions under "Frying Fritters" at the start of this section.
2. Allow to cool, then press each fritter between the palms of your hands to flatten. As you do this, the batter coating will break and reveal parts of the florets. Refry the dense florets in hot oil until the pakoras are lightly browned and crisp, approximately a minute or two. Drain using paper towels. Move all the fried pakoras to a serving platter, sprinkle the chaat masala on top, and serve.

EGGPLANT FRITTERS Ⓥ

This recipe is called "Baingan kae pakorae" in Hindi

Yield: 35 to 40 pieces

Ingredients:

- ¼ cup finely chopped fresh cilantro, including soft stems
- ¼ cup mustard oil
- ½ tablespoon Basic Garlic Paste (Homemade or store-bought)
- ½ teaspoon crudely ground ajwain seeds
- ½ teaspoon hot red pepper flakes, or to taste
- 1 recipe Basic Batter for Pakora Fritters
- 1 teaspoon Chaat Masala (Homemade or store-bought)
- 1½ to 2 cups peanut oil for deep-frying
- 2 Chinese eggplants, each 7 to 8 inches long and 2-inches in diameter, cut in ¼-inch-thick diagonal slices

Directions:

1. Ready the chaat masala and ginger-garlic paste. Next, ready the basic batter. Stir in the cilantro, garlic paste, ajwain seeds, and red pepper flakes. Put in the eggplant slices to the batter.
2. Fry using the directions under "Frying Fritters" at the start of this section. Move all the fried pakoras to a serving platter, sprinkle the chaat masala on top, and serve.

FRESH GREEN BEAN PAKORA FRITTERS

Ⓥ

This recipe is called "Hari phalliyon kae pakorae" in Hindi

Yield: 40 to 50 fritters

Ingredients:

- ½ teaspoon Chaat Masala (Homemade or store-bought)
- ½ teaspoon crushed ajwain seeds
- ½ teaspoon ground cumin

- 1 recipe Basic Batter for Pakora Fritters
- 1 tablespoon peeled and finely minced or ground fresh ginger
- 1 teaspoon ground coriander
- 1½ to 2 cups oil for deep-frying
- 40 to 50 fresh green beans (about ½ pound), trimmed from the stem end only

Directions:

1. Ready the chaat masala. Ready the basic batter. Stir in the coriander, cumin, ajwain seeds, and ginger. Put in the beans to the batter. Fry using the directions under "Frying Fritters" at the start of this section.
2. Move all the fried pakoras to a serving platter, sprinkle the chaat masala on top, and serve.

POTATO FRITTERS Ⓥ

This recipe is called "Aalu kae pakorae" in Hindi

Yield: 25 to 30 fritters

Ingredients:

- ½ teaspoon Chaat Masala (Homemade or store-bought)
- 1 recipe Basic Batter for Pakora Fritters
- 1 teaspoon crudely ground cumin or ajwain seeds
- 1½ to 2 cups oil for deep-frying
- 2 tablespoons minced chives
- 2 teaspoons ground coriander
- 3 to 4 small russet (or any) potatoes, thinly chopped

Directions:

1. Ready the chaat masala. Ready the basic batter. Stir in the coriander, cumin (or ajwain), and chives. Put in the potato slices in the batter.
2. Fry using the directions under "Frying Fritters" at the start of this section. Move all the fried pakoras to a serving platter, sprinkle the chaat masala on top, and serve.

PUMPKIN FRITTERS Ⓥ

This recipe is called "Pethae kae pakorae" in Hindi

Yield: 24 pieces

Ingredients:

- ½ teaspoon Chaat Masala (Homemade or store-bought)
- 1 (2- by 6-inch) piece pumpkin or butternut squash, cut into ¼-inch-thick slices
- 1 recipe Basic Batter for Pakora Fritters
- 1 teaspoon sugar
- 1½ to 2 cups peanut oil for deep-frying
- 2 teaspoons Bengali 5-Spices (Panch-Phoran) or store-bought

Directions:

1. Ready the chaat masala and the 5-spices. Next, ready the basic batter and stir in the 5-spices and the sugar.
2. Put in the pumpkin slices to the batter. Fry using the directions under "Frying Fritters" at the start of this section. Move all the fried pakoras to a serving platter, sprinkle the chaat masala on top, and serve.

SPINACH FRITTERS Ⓥ

This recipe is called "Palak kae pakorae" in Hindi

Yield: 50 to 60 pieces

Ingredients:

- ½ teaspoon crudely ground ajwain seeds
- ½ teaspoon hot red pepper flakes, or to taste
- ½ to 2 cups peanut oil for deep-frying
- 1 recipe Basic Batter for Pakora Fritters
- 1 teaspoon Basic Garlic Paste (Homemade or store-bought)
- 1 teaspoon Chaat Masala (Homemade or store-bought)

- 2 teaspoons ground coriander
- 50 to 60 baby spinach leaves with stems (about ½ pound)

Directions:

1. Ready the garlic paste and the chaat masala. Ready the basic batter. Stir in the garlic paste, coriander, ajwain seeds, and red pepper flakes. Put in the spinach to the batter.
2. Fry using the directions under "Frying Fritters" at the start of this section. Move all the fried pakoras to a serving platter, sprinkle the chaat masala on top, and serve.

STUFFED BREAD FRITTERS Ⓥ

This recipe is called "Bread pakorae" in Hindi

Yield: 24 pieces

Ingredients:

- ¼ teaspoon ground asafoetida
- ¼ teaspoon ground fenugreek seeds
- ½ cup or more any Coconut Chutney
- ½ teaspoon crudely ground black mustard seeds
- ½ teaspoon Chaat Masala (Homemade or store-bought)
- 1 cup peanut oil for deep-frying
- 1 recipe Basic Batter for Pakora Fritters
- 1 tablespoon minced fresh curry leaves
- 12 thin slices packaged white or whole-wheat bread, with or without crusts removed

Directions:

1. Ready the chaat masala and the coconut chutney. Ready the batter. Put the basic batter in a flat-bottomed dish and stir in the mustard and fenugreek seeds, curry leaves, and asafoetida.
2. Spread the coconut chutney liberally on 6 of the bread slices and cover with the rest of the 6 slices. Cut each "sandwich" into 4 squares or triangles.

3. Heat the oil in a big skillet (not a wok) until it reaches 350°F to 375°F on a frying thermometer, or a piece of bread dropped into the hot oil bubbles and surges to the surface of the oil instantly.
4. Cautiously, dip each square (or triangle) into the batter and add it to the hot oil, adding as many as the skillet can hold simultaneously. Fry, turning as required, until a golden colour is achieved on both sides, approximately two minutes.
5. Drain using paper towels. Move to a serving platter. Sprinkle with the chaat masala and serve.

SHREDDED AND MINCED VEGETABLE FRITTERS

CHOPPED ONION FRITTERS Ⓥ

This recipe is called "Kattae pyaz kae pakorae" in Hindi

Yield: 25 to 30 pieces

Ingredients:

- ¼ teaspoon baking soda
- ½ cup chickpea flour
- ½ cup finely chopped fresh cilantro, including soft stems
- ½ teaspoon Chaat Masala (Homemade or store-bought)
- ½ teaspoon ground ajwain seeds
- ½ teaspoon ground cumin
- 1 small onion, finely chopped or minced
- 1 small russet (or any) potato, peeled and grated
- 1 tablespoon peeled and finely chopped fresh ginger
- 1 teaspoon dried fenugreek leaves
- 1 teaspoon salt, or to taste
- 1½ to 2 cups peanut oil for deep-frying

- 2 teaspoons coriander, crudely crushed with the back of a spoon
- 2 to 3 tablespoons water

Directions:

1. Ready the chaat masala. Sieve the chickpea flour in a moderate-sized container and stir in the onion, potato, ginger, coriander, fenugreek, cumin, ajwain seeds, baking soda, and salt. Put in the water as required to make a semi-thick mixture.
2. Heat the oil as per directions under the "Frying Fritters" heading at the start of this section. Cautiously, using your fingers or a tablespoon, drop 1-inch uneven balls of the mixture cautiously into the hot oil and fry as directed at the start of this section. Move all the fried pakoras to a serving platter, sprinkle the chaat masala on top before you serve.

FENUGREEK FRITTERS Ⓥ

This recipe is called "Hari methi kae pakorae" in Hindi

Yield: 25 to 30 pieces

Ingredients:

- ⅛ teaspoon baking soda
- ½ cup chickpea flour
- ½ teaspoon <u>Chaat Masala</u> (Homemade or store-bought)
- ½ teaspoon salt, or to taste
- 1 tablespoon ground pomegranate seeds
- 1 teaspoon mango powder
- 1 to 3 fresh green chile peppers, such as serrano, minced with seeds
- 1½ to 2 cups peanut oil for deep frying
- 2 cups finely chopped fresh fenugreek leaves, including soft stems
- 2 tablespoons crudely ground coriander

Directions:

1. Ready the chaat masala. Put the chopped fenugreek leaves in a container and add all the other ingredients, except the oil and chaat masala and mix

thoroughly to make a semi-thick mixture, and set aside, approximately twenty minutes. Do not add any water; the washed leaves will be moist and the salt and spices will cause them to release more.

2. Heat the oil as per directions under the "Frying Fritters" heading at the start of this section. Cautiously, using your fingers or a tablespoon, drop 1-inch uneven balls of the mixture into the hot oil and fry as directed at the start of this section. Move all the pakoras to a serving platter, sprinkle the chaat masala on top before you serve.

MIXED VEGETABLE FRITTERS Ⓥ

This recipe is called "Milli-julli sabziyon kae pakorae" in Hindi

Yield: 25 to 30 pieces

Ingredients:

- ¼ teaspoon baking soda
- ½ cup each minced onion, red bell pepper
- ½ cup each: grated carrots, broccoli, potatoes, zucchini
- ½ cup finely chopped fresh cilantro, including soft stems
- ½ teaspoon crudely ground ajwain seeds
- ½ teaspoon crudely ground black pepper
- ½ to 2 cups oil for deep-frying
- 1 cup chickpea flour (besan), or more as required
- 1 cup finely chopped fresh spinach leaves
- 1 tablespoon peeled and minced fresh ginger
- 1 teaspoon Chaat Masala (Homemade or store-bought)
- 1 teaspoon salt, or to taste
- 1 to 3 fresh green chile peppers, such as serrano, minced with seeds

Directions:

1. Ready the chaat masala. In a container, mix everything except the oil and chaat masala together to make a semi-thick mixture, adding more chickpea flour if the batter appears too soft or some water if firm.
2. Heat the oil as per directions under the "Frying Fritters" heading at the start of this section. Cautiously, using clean fingers or a spoon, drop 1-inch balls of the

mixture into the hot oil and fry as directed at the start of this section. Move fritters to a platter, sprinkle with the chaat masala before you serve.

RICE FLOUR AND CASHEW FRITTERS Ⓥ

This recipe is called "Chaval atta aur kaaju kae pakorae" in Hindi

Yield: 15 to 20 pieces

Ingredients:

- ⅛ teaspoon baking soda
- ¼ cup chickpea flour
- ⅓ cup rice flour
- ½ cup crudely chopped fresh cilantro, including soft stems
- ½ teaspoon salt, or to taste
- 1 cup raw cashews
- 1 fresh green chile pepper, such as serrano, stemmed
- 1 small onion, crudely chopped
- 1½ to 2 cups peanut oil for deep frying
- 2 to 3 cups shredded lettuce (any kind)
- 4 to 6 quarter-size slices of peeled fresh ginger
- 8 to 10 fresh spinach leaves, with stems

Directions:

1. Using a food processor, combine and pulse the ginger, green chile pepper, onion, cilantro, and spinach until minced. Put in the cashews and pulse until the nuts are crudely chopped. Move to a container. Stir in the rice and chickpea flours, salt, and baking soda.
2. Heat the oil per directions under the "Frying Fritters" heading at the start of this section. Cautiously, using clean fingers or a spoon, drop 3/4- to 1-inch balls of the mixture into the hot oil and fry as directed at the start of this section. Move to paper towels to drain. Next, serve on a platter lined with shredded lettuce.

RICE FLOUR PAPAYA FRITTERS Ⓥ

This recipe is called "Chaval atta aur papitae kae pakorae" in Hindi

Yield: 35 to 40 pieces

Ingredients:

- ⅛ teaspoon baking soda
- ¼ teaspoon ground asafoetida
- ½ cup crudely chopped fresh cilantro, including soft stems
- ½ cup chickpea flour
- ½ teaspoon salt, or to taste
- ⅔ cup rice flour
- 1 small onion, crudely chopped
- 1 tablespoon crudely ground dried curry leaves
- 1 tablespoon vegetable oil
- 1 teaspoon mustard seeds
- 1 to 3 fresh green chile peppers, such as serrano, stemmed
- 1½ cups peeled and chopped firm unripe papaya
- 1½ to 2 cups peanut oil for deep-frying
- 2 tablespoons fresh lemon juice
- 2 to 3 cups shredded lettuce (any kind)
- 4 to 6 quarter-size slices peeled fresh ginger
- twelve to fifteen fresh spinach leaves, with stems

Directions:

1. Using a food processor, mix together and pulse the ginger, green chile peppers, onion, cilantro, spinach, and lemon juice until just minced. (Do not purée.) Put in the papaya and pulse until crudely chopped (do not mince). Move to a container. Put in the rice and chickpea flours, salt, and baking soda and mix thoroughly to make a thick, almost dough-like mixture. Add some more rice or chickpea flour, if required.
2. Heat 1 tablespoon oil in a small-sized non-stick sauce-pan using moderate to high heat and put in the mustard seeds and asafoetida. They should splutter when they touch the hot oil, so cover the pan and reduce the heat until the spluttering diminishes. Swiftly put in the curry leaves, stir for approximately half a minute, then mix the spices into the mixture.

3. Heat the peanut oil as per directions under the "Frying Fritters" heading at the start of this section. Divide the mixture into 12 identical portions and form into rolls or cylinders, each approximately 1 inch thick and 3 inches long (they don't have to be smooth). Cautiously slide them into the hot oil, adding as many as the wok can hold simultaneously without crowding, and fry, turning and moving them around as required until a golden colour is achieved, approximately two to three minutes.

4. Move with slotted spatula to paper towels to drain. Once cool sufficient to hold, pinch off approximately 1-inch pieces from each roll and refry in hot oil, drain on paper towels again, then serve on a bed of shredded lettuce.

SHREDDED CABBAGE FRITTERS

This recipe is called "Bundh gobhi kae pakorae" in Hindi

Yield: 30 to 40 pieces

Ingredients:

- ¼ cup finely chopped fresh cilantro, including soft stems
- ¼ teaspoon baking soda
- ¼ to ⅓ cup non-fat plain yogurt, whisked until the desired smoothness is achieved
- ½ teaspoon crudely ground ajwain seeds
- ½ teaspoon Chaat Masala
- 1 fresh green chile pepper, such as serrano, minced with seeds
- 1 tablespoon ground coriander
- 1 tablespoon peeled and minced fresh ginger
- 1 teaspoon dried fenugreek leaves
- 1 teaspoon salt, or to taste
- 1 to 1½ cups chickpea flour (besan)
- 1½ cups finely shredded or chopped cabbage or Brussels sprouts (or mixed)
- 1½ to 2 cups mustard or peanut oil for deep-frying

Directions:

1. 1. Ready the chaat masala. In a container, combine all the ingredients, except the oil and chaat masala to make a semi-thick mixture, adding more chickpea

flour if the mixture appears too soft or some water if it is too firm. Let sit for about fifteen to twenty minutes.

2. **2.** Heat the oil as per directions under the "Frying Fritters" heading at the start of this section. Cautiously, using your fingers or a tablespoon, drop 1-inch uneven balls of the mixture cautiously into the hot oil and fry as directed at the start of this section. Move all the fried pakoras to a serving platter, sprinkle the chaat masala on top before you serve.

SPLIT PEA FRITTERS Ⓥ

This recipe is called "Muttar dal kae pakorae" in Hindi

Yield: 20 to 25 pieces

Ingredients:

- ¼ teaspoon baking soda
- ½ cup crudely chopped fresh cilantro, including soft stems
- ½ cup green split peas (muttar dal), sorted and washed in 3 to 4 changes of water
- ½ teaspoon crudely ground ajwain seeds
- ½ teaspoon <u>Chaat Masala</u>or store-bought)
- ½ teaspoon ground cumin
- ⅔ cup chickpea flour, or more as required
- 1 cup crudely chopped cooking greens, your choice, such as radish, spinach, daikon, or mustard
- 1 small green bell pepper, crudely chopped
- 1 small onion, crudely chopped
- 1 small russet (or any) potato, crudely chopped
- 1 teaspoon ground dried oregano
- 1 teaspoon salt, or to taste
- 1 to 3 fresh green chile peppers, such as serrano, stemmed
- 1½ tablespoons ground coriander
- 2 small carrots, crudely chopped
- 2 to 3 cups peanut oil for deep-frying
- 5 quarter-size slices peeled fresh ginger

Directions:

1. Ready the chaat masala. Immerse the split peas in water to cover by 2 inches, approximately four hours, then drain.
2. Using a food processor, mix together and pulse the ginger, green chile and bell peppers, onion, potato, carrots, greens, and half the split peas until just minced. (Do not over-process into a purée.) Move to a container, stir in the rest of the split peas, all the spices, baking soda, and salt. Next, Put in the chickpea flour and mix thoroughly to make a semi-thick mixture. If the mixture appears too soft add more chickpea flour, and if it appears too dry add some water, and mix once more.
3. Heat the oil as per directions under the "Frying Fritters" heading at the start of this section. Cautiously, using clean fingers or a spoon, drop 1-inch balls of the mixture into the hot oil and fry as directed at the start of this section. Move to a platter, sprinkle with the chaat masala before you serve.

CHEESE AND MEAT FRITTERS

CHICKEN FRITTERS

This recipe is called "Murgh kae pakorae" in Hindi

Yield: ten to fifteen pieces

Ingredients:

- ½ teaspoon crudely ground ajwain seeds
- ½ teaspoon Chaat Masala (Homemade or store-bought)
- ½ teaspoon hot red pepper flakes, or to taste
- ½ teaspoon salt, or to taste
- 1 (2½- to 3-pound) chicken, skinned and cut into serving pieces (discard the back and wings)
- 1 recipe Basic Batter for Pakora Fritters
- 1 tablespoon ground coriander

- 1 teaspoon dry-roasted and crudely ground cumin seeds (See the dry-roasting section in Introduction)
- 1 teaspoon garam masala
- 1 teaspoon ground cumin seeds
- 1½ to 2 cups peanut oil for deep-frying
- 2 cups water
- 2 tablespoons Basic Ginger-Garlic Paste (Homemade or store-bought)
- 2 tablespoons minced fresh cilantro, including soft stems

Directions:

1. Ready the ginger-garlic paste. Next, place the chicken, water, ginger-garlic paste, garam masala, and salt in a small saucepan and bring to a boil using high heat. Reduce the heat to moderate to low, cover the pan and simmer until the chicken is tender and all the water has been absorbed, fifteen to twenty minutes. If the chicken cooks before the water dries up, uncover the pan and cook until the chicken is completely dry. Allow to cool, remove the bones and cut into smaller pieces, if you wish.
2. In the meantime, ready the chaat masala and the dry-roasted cumin seeds. Next, ready the basic batter, and stir in the cilantro, coriander, cumin, red pepper flakes, and ajwain seeds.
3. Put in the chicken to the batter. Heat the oil and fry the chicken as per directions under the "Frying Fritters" heading at the start of this section. Move to a platter, sprinkle with the roasted cumin and chaat masala.

FISH FRITTERS

This recipe is called "Macchi kae pakorae" in Hindi

Yield: twelve to fifteen pieces

Ingredients:

- ⅛ teaspoon ground asafoetida
- ½ teaspoon crudely ground ajwain seeds
- ½ teaspoon ground turmeric
- ½ teaspoon hot red pepper flakes, or to taste
- ½ teaspoon salt, or to taste

- 1 recipe Basic Batter for Pakora Fritters
- 1 teaspoon Chaat Masala (Homemade or store-bought)
- 1 teaspoon ground cumin
- 1¼ pounds halibut, salmon or sea bass fillets, approximately 1 inch thick, cut into 1½-inch pieces
- 1½ to 2 cups oil for deep-frying
- 2 large cloves garlic, finely ground
- 2 tablespoons chickpea or rice flour
- 2 tablespoons finely chopped fresh cilantro leaves
- 2 to 3 scallions, green parts only, minced
- 3 tablespoons distilled white vinegar

Directions:

1. Ready the chaat masala. Put the fish pieces in a container. Put in the vinegar, garlic, red pepper flakes, turmeric, and salt, and mix thoroughly, ensuring all the pieces are coated thoroughly. Cover and marinate at least 1 and up to 3 hours in a fridge.
2. Ready the basic batter, then stir in the flour, cumin, ajwain, asafoetida, and scallion greens. Heat the oil as per directions under the "Frying Fritters" heading at the start of this section. Dip each fish piece in the batter to cover thoroughly and fry as directed at the start of this section. Move to a platter, sprinkle with the chaat masala and cilantro before you serve.

GROUND MEAT FRITTERS

This recipe is called "Keema pakorae" in Hindi

Yield: 20 to 25 pieces

Ingredients:

- ¼ teaspoon ground turmeric
- ½ cup crudely chopped fresh cilantro, including soft stems
- ½ teaspoon Chaat Masala (Homemade or store-bought)
- ½ teaspoon salt, or to taste
- 1 large fresh garlic clove, peeled
- 1 pound extra lean ground meat (beef or lamb)

- 1 recipe Basic Batter for Pakora Fritters
- 1 small onion, crudely chopped
- 1 tablespoon dried fenugreek leaves
- 1 teaspoon garam masala
- 1 to 3 fresh green chile peppers, such as serrano, stemmed
- 1½ to 2 cups oil for deep-frying
- 2 tablespoons rice flour
- 3 to 4 slices packaged white or whole-wheat bread (crusts on or not)
- 4 to 6 quarter-size slices peeled fresh ginger

Directions:

1. Ready the chaat masala. Immerse the bread in water to cover approximately one minute. Next, squeeze out all the water and crudely crumble the bread.
2. Using a food processor, combine and pulse the crumbled bread, onion, cilantro, ginger, garlic, and green chile peppers until minced. Put in the ground meat, fenugreek leaves, garam masala, and salt, and process once more to mix thoroughly. Divide into 20 to 25 portions and shape each one into a 2-inch disc.
3. Ready the basic batter and stir in the rice flour and turmeric. Heat the oil as per directions under the "Frying Fritters" heading at the start of this section. Dip each disc in the batter to coat well, and fry as directed at the start of this section. Move to a platter, sprinkle with the chaat masala before you serve.

MARINATED CHICKEN PAKORA FRITTERS

This recipe is called "Murgh pakorae" in Hindi

Yield: 20 to 24 pieces

Ingredients:

- ¼ cup non-fat plain yogurt, whisked until the desired smoothness is achieved
- ½ small onion, crudely chopped
- ½ teaspoon Chaat Masala (Homemade or store-bought)
- ½ teaspoon salt, or to taste
- 1 large clove garlic, peeled

- 1 recipe Basic Batter for Pakora Fritters
- 1 tablespoon fresh lime or lemon juice
- 1 teaspoon garam masala
- 1 to 2 tablespoons rice flour
- 1 to 3 fresh green chile peppers, such as serrano, stemmed
- 10 to 12 chicken breast tenders, each cut along the diagonal in half
- 1½ to 2 cups peanut oil for deep frying
- 4 quarter-size slices peeled fresh ginger

Directions:

1. Using a food processor or a blender, combine and pulse the onion, ginger, garlic, and chile peppers until minced. Next, Put in the yogurt, lime juice, oil, garam masala, and salt, and process until the desired smoothness is achieved. Move to a moderate-sized container. Put in the chicken and mix until all the pieces are fully coated with the mixture. Cover and marinate at least 4 and up to 24 hours in a fridge.
2. Ready the chaat masala and the basic batter. Bring the chicken to room temperature, then mix it into the pakora batter along with the rice flour.
3. Heat the oil and fry the chicken as per directions under the "Frying Fritters" heading at the start of this section. You can fry just once, but for the best flavour and texture, allow to cool down, then refry in hot oil until heated through. Move to paper towels once more. Sprinkle with the chaat masala and serve.

PANEER FRITTERS

This recipe is called Ppaneer pakorae" in Hindi

Yield: 20 pieces

Ingredients:

- ¼ cup minced fresh cilantro, including soft stems
- ½ teaspoon crudely ground ajwain seeds
- 1 recipe
- 1 teaspoon Chaat Masala (Homemade or store-bought)
- 1 to 3 fresh green chile peppers, such as serrano, minced with seeds

- 1½ to 2 cups peanut oil for deep-frying
- 8 ounces (1 recipe) <u>Paneer Cheese</u> (Homemade or store-bought)

Directions:

1. Ready the paneer cheese, then the chaat masala. Slice the paneer cheese into pieces or place into a food processor and process until it begins to gather into a dough. Move it to a cutting board and shape into a large square or rectangle and cut into 20 ½-by-2-inch rectangles.
2. Ready the basic fritter batter. To the batter, stir in the cilantro, green chile peppers, and ajwain seeds. Heat the oil as per directions under the "Frying Fritters" heading at the start of this section. Dip each paneer cheese rectangle into the batter to cover thoroughly and fry as directed at the start of this section. Move to a platter, sprinkle with the chaat masala before you serve.

PANEER FRITTERS WITH GREEN CHUTNEY

This recipe is called "Paneer aur hari chutni kae pakorae" in Hindi

Yield: Approximately 30 pieces

Ingredients:

- ¼ cup rice flour, or more as required
- ½ cup Basic Green Chutney
- 1 recipe Basic Batter for Pakora Fritters
- 1 teaspoon <u>Chaat Masala</u> (Homemade or store-bought)
- 1½ to 2 cups peanut oil for deep-frying
- 8 ounces (1 recipe) <u>Paneer Cheese</u> (Homemade or store-bought), crudely crumbled

Directions:

1. Ready the chaat masala, paneer chese, and the green chutney. In a container, toss together the paneer cheese and the chutney and marinate one to two hours at room temperature.

2. Ready the pakora batter, stir in the rice flour, then Put in the marinated paneer cheese (plus the marinade) and 1 tablespoon of the oil to make a semi-thick mixture.
3. Heat the oil as per directions under the "Frying Fritters" heading at the start of this section. Cautiously, with your clean fingers or a spoon, drop 1-inch balls of the mixture into the hot oil and fry as directed at the start of this section. Move to a platter, sprinkle with the chaat masala before you serve.

PANEER FRITTERS WITH RED BELL PEPPERS

This recipe is called "Paneer aur laal shimla mirch kae pakorae" in Hindi

Yield: 20 to 25 pieces

Ingredients:

- ¼ cup finely chopped scallions, green parts only
- ¼ teaspoon salt, or to taste
- ½ cup large curd cottage cheese
- ½ teaspoon Chaat Masala (Homemade or store-bought)
- ⅔ cup chickpea flour, or more as required
- 1 red bell pepper, minced
- 1 small russet (or any) potato, grated
- 1 tablespoon peeled and minced fresh ginger
- 1 teaspoon ground coriander
- 1 to 3 fresh green chile peppers, such as serrano, minced with seeds
- 1½ to 2 cups peanut oil for deep-frying

Directions:

1. Ready the chaat masala. In a moderate-sized container, combine all the ingredients (except the oil and chaat masala) to make a thick, dough-like batter. (If the batter is too soft, add a little more chickpea flour.) Divide into 20 to 25 uneven balls.

2. Heat the oil as per directions under the "Frying Fritters" heading at the start of this section, cautiously drop the balls into the hot oil and fry as directed at the start of this section.

3. Allow to cool, then press them lightly between the palms of your hands into small discs with ragged edges. Refry them in hot oil until crisp, approximately two to three minutes. Drain using paper towels, move to a platter, sprinkle with the chaat masala before you serve.

SHRIMP FRITTERS

This recipe is called "Jhingae kae pakorae" in Hindi

Yield: 15 to 20 pieces

Ingredients:

- ¼ cup finely chopped fresh cilantro, including soft stems
- ½ teaspoon crudely ground ajwain seeds
- ½ teaspoon ground turmeric
- ½ teaspoon hot red pepper flakes, or to taste
- ½ teaspoon salt, or to taste
- 1 recipe Basic Batter for Pakora Fritters, made with yogurt instead of water
- 1 teaspoon crudely ground cumin seeds
- 1 teaspoon Chaat Masala (Homemade or store-bought)
- 1½ to 2 cups oil for deep-frying
- 15 to 20 fresh jumbo shrimp (about 1 pound), shelled and deveined, with tails on
- 2 large cloves fresh garlic, peeled and minced
- 2 to 3 tablespoons fresh lime or lemon juice

Directions:

1. Ready the chaat masala. Put the shrimp in a container. Put in the lime juice, garlic, turmeric, red pepper flakes, ajwain, and salt, and mix thoroughly, ensuring all the pieces coated thoroughly. Cover and marinate at least 1 and up to 3 hours in a fridge.

2. Ready the basic batter, using yogurt instead of water, then stir in the cumin and cilantro. Heat the oil as per directions under the "Frying Fritters" heading

at the start of this section. Dip each shrimp in the batter to cover thoroughly and fry as directed at the start of this section. Move to a platter, sprinkle with the chaat masala before you serve.

ENDNOTE

Thank you for the valuable time you spend on my book. I hope it helped you at least a little, making you a slightly better Indian cook, at least. Every little bit counts! If you liked this book, don't forget to check out other books on Indian Cooking by Rekha Sharma!

Printed in Great Britain
by Amazon